William Tyndale

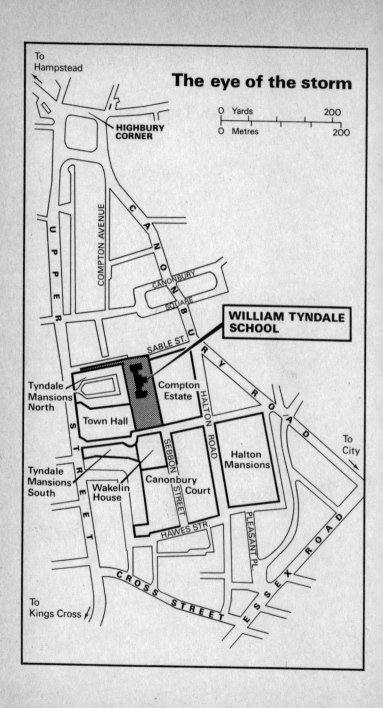

The eye of the storm

To Hampstead

HIGHBURY CORNER

Yards 0 — 200
Metres 0 — 200

COMPTON AVENUE

CANONBURY

CANONBURY SQUARE

SABLE ST.

WILLIAM TYNDALE SCHOOL

UPPER STREET

Tyndale Mansions North

Town Hall

Compton Estate

HALTON ROAD

CANONBURY ROAD

Tyndale Mansions South

Wakelin House

Canonbury Court

SEBBON STREET

Halton Mansions

To City

HAWES STR.

PLEASANT PL.

CROSS STREET

ESSEX ROAD

To Kings Cross

William Tyndale

Collapse of a School – or a System?

John Gretton

Mark Jackson

London
George Allen & Unwin Ltd
Ruskin House, Museum Street

ISBN Cased edition   0 04 371047 6
      Paperback edition   0 04 371048 4

Cover design by Les Lawrence

Made and printed in Great Britain
in 10 point Times New Roman
by William Clowes & Sons, Limited
London, Beccles and Colchester

Foreword

In the autumn of 1973 William Tyndale was an ordinary enough junior school in a rundown area of north London; within just two years the school had fallen apart and striking teachers, angry parents and helpless politicians were confronting one another through the headlines of the national press and the current affairs programmes of television. It took a further year, which must have seemed to many of those directly concerned to have lasted as long as the previous two, for the inquiry to be completed and its report published and, in a further blaze of publicity, for the leading politicians and the more active of the school's managers to resign while the headteacher and five of his colleagues prepared to face disciplinary proceedings.

It was unheard of for a primary school to attract so much attention. Universities or colleges of art might, from time to time, be occupied or otherwise brought to a halt; secondary schools, in the glare of political controversy, might sometimes attract public notice as one or other of them sank into urban deprivation, vandalism and academic failure. But primary schools were the bedrock of the education system. Indeed, the English primary school at its best had a worldwide reputation. Yet the disintegration of William Tyndale could scarcely have occurred more quickly or more thoroughly if it had been brought about by its own pupils trained in the techniques of subversion.

The story of that disintegration makes a fascinating educational whodunit in its own right, and we sketch in the main outlines in the first chapter, coming back to fill in bits of detail here and there later on. As a detective story, it is one of the psychological sort where there are no heroes and too many 'villains', all of varying shades of grey. For the real interest of William Tyndale lies only partly in sorting out heroes and villains. Of equal importance is the threat its collapse posed (simply by imposing it to public scrutiny) to the whole system – i.e. to the delicate interlocking relationships of teachers, headmaster, parents, managers, local education authority administrators and inspectors, politicians, teacher unions and the Secretary of State and the Department of Education and Science.

5

Thus even the briefest account of the story must raise the question: which was more to blame – the disarray of the teachers, the Machiavellian tactics of some of the managers, or the impotence and inadequacy of the Inner London Education Authority's political and bureaucratic machinery? And simply to ask the question leads us straight from the school into the system. Moreover, as a result of the inquiry which was set up following the school's collapse, and of the way in which that inquiry was conducted over four months, we are uniquely well placed to look at that system. Nowhere else, we are sure, has such a mass of documentary and verbal evidence on the workings of one school been accumulated and made available to the interested public. Much of that evidence was summarised in the official report of the inquiry, which was primarily concerned with who said and did what to whom. Our concerns have been wider, and we have not only made use of all the evidence given to the inquiry, but we have talked to other people who were not called as witnesses – the teachers who taught the William Tyndale teachers, for example.

As always in education, everybody claimed to be acting from the best of motives: the good of the children (though as usual when their good is discussed, the children themselves were left on the sidelines). One of the questions we examine is, which children's good – all children's, some children's, one's own child's? There was little clear idea, either, of what 'good' meant in that context. From an outsider's point of view, it might seem a simple matter to determine what should be taught in primary schools. In practice, it is not, and this lack of formal agreement was at the heart of the matter. Obviously, there is a wide area of consensus; otherwise children would not be happily spending four of the best years of their lives at junior schools up and down the country without all of them turning into William Tyndales. But when an unspoken agreement collapses, then all sides have a vested interest in arguing that their own view of what ought to have been happening was the right one. That is why William Tyndale has proved such a fascinating case study: the issues were forced into the open – what should be taught, how it should be taught and who should see that it is taught. The disagreements became clear for all to see and, by the same token, highlighted the ineffectual controls.

At the very least, we hope that all who read this book will realise that everybody – and not just parents or children – is a 'consumer' of education and has a right to know, and ask questions about, what goes on in our schools. We hope too that they will have a clearer idea of what sorts of questions they can

6

reasonably ask of a headmaster and his staff, not to mention their elected representatives on the local education committee or their MPs.

Finally, a word about ourselves, together with the usual acknowledgements and disclaimers. We are, both of us, journalists first and foremost, and not educationists. That means that in the various minefields into which we have ventured, we may have occasionally trodden on something rather nasty; if so, we alone are to blame. But it has the advantage, we hope, that our approach and our concerns, free of the cant that bedevils so much thinking on education, will be shared by a wider audience. We owe a big debt of gratitude to the editor of *The Times Educational Supplement*, Stuart Maclure, not merely for giving us the time and resources to research and write this book but for his very practical help and advice. Above all, we would like to say thank you to Lois Rodgers. She did a great deal of invaluable research and, by diligent checking, eradicated scores of errors. This book is as much hers as ours.

London
August 1976

Contents

Foreword   5

1. An Unhappy School   15

2. The Islington Setting   27

3. The Heart of the Matter   37

4. Some Outside Influences   47

5. Representing the Community   61

6. Appointing and Politicking   69

7. A Divided Authority   77

8. A Look at the Inspectors   85

9. The Union's not their Leader   97

10. The 'Trial' of William Tyndale   105

    Epilogue   117

Throughout the book, in the context of William Tyndale, unless specified otherwise, the phrases Mr. Ellis and his colleagues, the teachers, the staff, are to be taken to refer to the following: Mr. Ellis, Mr. Haddow, Mr. Felton, Miss Green, Mrs. McColgan, Mrs. McWhirter, Miss Richards.

Those Involved

Alan Head	Headteacher of William Tyndale Junior School 1968–73
Jean Donnison	Chairman of managers until August 1973
Robin Auld, QC	Chairman of the inquiry
Brian Haddow	Teacher at William Tyndale Junior School
Terry Ellis	Headteacher of William Tyndale Junior School from January 1974
Irene Chowles	Deputy headteacher of William Tyndale Junior School since 1968
Jackie McWhirter	Teacher and NUT representative at William Tyndale Junior School
Dorothy McColgan	Teacher at William Tyndale Junior School
Dolly Walker	Part-time remedial teacher at William Tyndale Junior School until December 1974
Aelfthryth Gittings	Manager of William Tyndale
Denise Dewhurst	Junior parent manager of William Tyndale until July 1974
Stella Burnett	Chairman of managers until February 1975
Donald Rice	District inspector responsible for William Tyndale from March 1974
Harvey Hinds	Chairman of the ILEA schools sub-committee from 1970 until his resignation in July 1976
Anne Page	Islington borough councillor and the council's representative on the ILEA since May 1974; chairman of the council's education advisory committee since its inception in July 1975
Valeria Fairweather	Manager of William Tyndale
Robin Mabey	Manager of William Tyndale and Islington borough councillor for St Mary's ward since 1971
Brenda Hart	Headteacher of William Tyndale Infant School
David Austin	Teacher at William Tyndale Junior School, 1974–5

Elisabeth Hoodless	Manager of William Tyndale from January 1975
Brian Tennant	Manager of William Tyndale and chairman since February 1975
Laurie Buxton	Former district inspector responsible for William Tyndale, now staff inspector (mathematics)
Peter Newsam	Deputy education officer of the ILEA since 1972 and successor to Dr Briault on his retirement in January 1977
Eric Briault	Chief education officer of the ILEA since 1971
Donald Hoodless	Deputy leader of the Islington borough council and St Mary's ward councillor
Alan Pedrick	St Mary's ward councillor since 1974
Jenny Baker	Opposition leader on the schools sub-committee and Islington councillor from 1968–71
Sir Ashley Bramall	Leader of the ILEA since 1970
Patricia Burgess	Senior assistant education officer (primary) since 1973
Stephen Sedley	Counsel for the teachers
Edward Davidson	Counsel for the ILEA
Tessa Moorhouse	Counsel for the managers
John Williams	Counsel for Mrs Walker

1. An Unhappy School

Happy schools, like happy families, are similar and unremarkable. It is only unhappy ones that attract the attention of the novelist or the journalist. When in July 1973 Alan Head left William Tyndale Junior School, after five years as headmaster, most people would have classed it as a happy school. Some of the teachers were inclined to dispute that and, with the benefit of hindsight, it might just have been possible to detect signs of the unhappiness to come; but such signs as there were remained well hidden at the end of that summer term.

Yet the material with which Mr Head had to work was as unpromising as any in London. Built in 1916, when schools still seemed to have been designed on much the same lines as prisons, William Tyndale conformed by and large to the general pattern: three storeys high, each consisting of a corridor with enclosed classrooms on one side and assembly/dining halls, kitchens, staffrooms and offices on the other. The ground floor was for the infant school (5 to 7 year olds), with its own headteacher; the remaining two floors were for the juniors. There was a small asphalt-covered area that bore the courtesy title of a playground. Such schools were built to cater for the children of industrial, working-class communities, so William Tyndale was surrounded by blocks of council flats, some small factories and, unusually, the back of Islington town hall.

Originally known as the Sebbon Street School, after one of the small streets at its back, its name was changed in 1949 following a directive from the then Ministry of Education; it was thought that schools named after streets were likely to categorise children who attended them for the rest of their lives as 'council children', and that this would be an undesirable stigma. The managing body at the time put forward the name of William Tyndale. This was thought to be a dual reference to a Colonel Tyndale, an eighteenth-century landowner who gave his name to some of the surrounding estates but appears to have left no record of his first name, and to the martyr of the Protestant Reformation and translator of the English bible.

The school was sandwiched between two main roads, which

the children inside had to cross to get out and those outside had to cross to get in. Once there was a link road by the school, joining the two main roads. But Sable Street had been cut off at one end, to form the principal entrance to the school. The rest of it had been divided into lanes, one running down to a block of flats, the other to the school, rather like a drive. But the drive was lined, not with trees, but with a high brick wall.

The environment might have been the same, but the community for which the school was designed had changed. Mr Head once described his school as consisting of a few children from middle-class families, a few from skilled or semi-skilled working-class ones and a great mass of deprived, many of whom were recent immigrants: West Indian, Asian or eastern Mediterranean. William Tyndale was certainly not alone in having among its intake a large proportion of the classic 'problem' children of today's inner city ghettos. And Mr Head was not alone in having welded out of all this a school which had an excellent reputation. A thin, eager, dynamic man, he was always about the school. He got on well with children, staff, parents and the head of the infant school. The teaching styles he encouraged were probably more 'progressive' than 'formal', but he was careful in his approach. He liked team-teaching, for example, but he saw to it that teams were formed only of teachers who were likely to work well together. With the usual high London turnover of staff, this was difficult; but with the help of Jean Donnison, his strong no-nonsense chairman of managers, Mr Head achieved for the school the sort of reputation for sympathetic tolerance combined with effective teaching that middle-class parents liked. And those middle-class parents showed their approval by putting William Tyndale second only to Canonbury School on their pecking order of desirable local schools for their offspring. When Mr Head left, William Tyndale was, to all outward appearances, a going conern, a happy school.

It was not long to remain so. Within a year, the staff were quarrelling among themselves about teaching methods, and the quarrel had become public and spread to include the parents. Within a further year, the teachers' disagreements and the parents' unease had been lifted on to a different plane by a politically active group of managers. It became an open conflict between most of the staff and this group of managers, with local and party political ramifications. The result was the disintegration of the school, a strike by the teachers and the mammoth inquiry by Robin Auld, QC.

The trouble might be said to have begun with one of the last

16

acts of Mr Head. In the April before he left he appointed Brian Haddow to the staff. Mr Haddow was an extremely gifted teacher, with strongly held views on the merits of, and need for, radically progressive classroom methods; he had the sort of charisma that makes people excellent teachers of children and leaders of their peers. Mr Head recognised his ability and thought his ideas would fit in with the team-teaching approach he was introducing into the school. If he foresaw difficulties, arising perhaps from the power of Mr Haddow's personality and his strongly held convictions, he must have thought that he could handle them, and that therefore – the sort of *non sequitur* that it is all too easy to make – whoever was appointed as his successor would be able to handle them.

However, when Terry Ellis finally arrived to take up his headship in January 1974, there were already indications that all would not be well. His appointment had been somewhat *faute de mieux*. The post had been advertised twice, once in the spring and again in the autumn; Mr Ellis had applied, and been interviewed, on both occasions. Small London primary schools did not then attract many very suitable candidates. The first time round, the managers were unable to recommend anybody; the second time, a rather different set of managers put forward Mr Ellis, though with some reservations.

The delay meant that there was an interregnum of one term – again, not an uncommon occurrence in London. The deputy head, Irene Chowles, acted as headteacher, but was not happy in the job. She had not applied for the post first time round, and talked about the difficulties she had in running the school in her interview when she did apply in the autumn. Her name was not among the three put forward to County Hall for the final decision, which is unusual when a deputy head applies. Some of the difficulties she encountered during that term could be traced to Mr Haddow who, though he had come to the school for the first time in September, was quickly appointed acting deputy head on the grounds that he was the only male full-time member of staff. Though disappointed by what he saw as the generally unprogressive nature of the teaching in the school, he made no startling innovations in that direction during his first term. He did, however, encourage his fourth-year class to hold weekly 'council meetings', and from these a number of doubtless irritating resolutions – on topics such as eating sweets and assembly – landed on Mrs Chowles's desk. Mr Haddow, together with Jackie McWhirter, who was to become the school's union representative, wrote to Mrs Chowles to say that the staff would no longer do dinner duty; as a result extra help had to be paid for out of money set aside for books and stationery. Dorothy McColgan, who was to join the staff two terms later, came to talk about her dispute with the ILEA; Mr Haddow was practically alone in wanting to sign a motion of support for her. Other difficulties included a first-year class that was divided between two part-time teachers who differed strongly on teaching methods; and a probationary teacher who was frequently absent from school because, as Mrs Chowles put it in her evidence to the inquiry, 'she was experiencing great difficulties with a class containing many highly disturbed children'.

Such is the daily round of many headteachers, and none of it would have worried one with the experience and personality of Mr Head. As it was, the effects of a term's interregnum were exacerbated. Given all that, one might have expected one of the ILEA's inspectors, many of whom are themselves ex-headteachers, to put in frequent appearances at the start of Mr Ellis's first term to lend support and advice until he and the school had settled down. However, there was also an interregnum in the office of the district inspector responsible, so for his first term at least Mr Ellis was left to cope largely on his own.

His first action, sensibly enough, was to institute regular staff meetings. However, in the minds of some of the staff, and possibly at times even in that of Mr Ellis, this was not just for the airing, and eventual resolving, of differences, but a first step in the withering away of the power of the head and its replacement by a genuine teachers' co-operative. However, it all happened rather more quickly than perhaps anyone could have anticipated. For in the summer term, Mrs McColgan, a well-known advocate of teachers' (as distinct from children's) rights, joined the staff, meetings became weekly and decisions were taken which were held to be as binding on the head as on anybody else. At the first sign of trouble the defensive vocabulary of a fledgeling political bureaucracy emerged: the 'validity' of decisions by others was questioned and 'procedures' were thrown into doubt. At least up to September 1974, though, a certain realism could sometimes prevail. Mr Ellis's role had been 'defined' by the co-operative so that he was little more than one member of it among others, but after he alone, and not the whole co-operative, had been summoned to divisional office, the staff 'redefined' his role nearer to the traditional one of a head; he kept his own room.

During that first term, Mr Ellis also agreed to give Mr Haddow a free rein in his own class, and Mr Haddow responded in kind with his children. This was the class that was to be at the centre of so much controversy later. They watched television or played

18

table-tennis at will; they disrupted the school routine (not to mention the cleaners) by coming into class early, staying late, ignoring break rules and wandering all over the building at will (they took to using the staff toilets). Children were attracted from other classes into Mr Haddow's. Exceptional teacher that he was, Mr Haddow was able to preserve enough order and provide enough stimulus for at least one parent to say later that their son 'had had a marvellous year, one that he would remember for the rest of his life'. Other teachers, who lacked Mr Haddow's charisma, tried to emulate his methods. To some teachers, though, and a growing number of parents, it began to seem as though there was neither order nor teaching in the school.

The school had a large number of poor readers, many of whom (80 out of 217) would have qualified for remedial teaching. Mr Ellis and the staff decided to institute a form of 'setting' for reading, known as vertical grouping. This meant forming the children into sets according to criteria other than age, such as reading ability, leaving a small number still to be taught by the half-time remedial teacher, Dolly Walker. Together with Mrs Chowles, the deputy head, Mrs Walker was strongly opposed to the way decisions were being taken in the staffroom and implemented in the school.

Mr Haddow had written to the parents of his class to explain the innovations he was introducing, but at the end of March Mr Ellis decided to hold a parents' meeting so that he could put across his reading scheme. This was an admirable idea in itself; the trouble was that Mr Ellis impressed at least one parent there as being rather confused about the aims of his scheme and how it would actually work. Some parents also voiced a more general dissatisfaction with the way the school was being run. A number of parents with children in the infant school had decided to send them somewhere else when Mr Head left, but now, for the first time, middle-class parents began to debate among themselves whether they should keep their children on at a school run by Mr Ellis. Most decided to give it another term.

But Mr Ellis did not get a second term to show what he and his staff could do. Barely two months later, in that first summer term, everything blew up in the teachers' faces, and the school began very quickly to fall apart. Parents' criticism of the school was becoming much more widespread and vociferous as they waited in the playground to collect their children. Two of the managers who had children at the school, Aelfthryth Gittings and Denise Dewhurst, the parent manager, were sufficiently concerned to report these criticisms to the chairman of the managers, Stella

Burnett, who arranged a meeting between the three of them and Mr Ellis and Mr Haddow, the teachers' representative on the managing body.

At about the same time, Mrs Walker, tired of being continually over-ruled in the staffroom and increasingly concerned that policies which other members of staff saw as being intended specifically to help the deprived were in fact detrimental to their education, like some cross between Luther and Zola, pinned her accusatory statement to the staff noticeboard – after giving a copy to Mr Ellis. Four pages long, the signed statement, entitled 'Commentary on William Tyndale School 22 May 1974', was trenchant, even vitriolic, in tone. Besides recounting all the criticisms which she and, to a lesser extent, Mrs Chowles had been making in staffroom discussions about the way the children were being taught, it referred to Mr Ellis as 'the biggest buck-passer I have ever met' and ended by threatening to call a parents' meeting herself to discuss the situation if Mr Ellis was not prepared to call one. The staff and Mr Ellis were furious with Mrs Walker. From that time on most of them were convinced that she had been to a large extent responsible for stirring up the parents against them, and suspicions of that sort of behind-the-scenes activity largely nullified any good that might have come out of the meeting between the three managers and Mr Ellis and Mr Haddow.

At this point, though, the staff were on the whole more concerned with money than with parents' reactions. It was the time of the campaign, supported by the ILEA and widespread throughout London's schools, for a bigger allowance to compensate for the high cost, particularly in terms of housing, of living and working in London. A strike had been called for 14 June, and the staff decided to call a parents' meeting for the day before to explain why they were striking and to get the parents' support, which they had no reason to think they would not get. Mrs Dewhurst and Mrs Gittings, the two managers with children in the school, had already collected signatures from nearly all the parents for a petition to John Grant, Labour MP for Islington Central. Mrs Dewhurst, according to one account, had even suggested in April that William Tyndale children join the staff in the protest march on Westminster by London parents and teachers that was led by Sir Ashley Bramall, chairman of the Inner London Education Authority.

That meeting, however, backfired. About forty-five parents turned up, and they made it plain that they were not, on the whole, interested in the London Allowance. Several angrily denounced the way the school was being run: it was not a question, they said, of how their children were being taught, but that they were not being taught at all. Calm was restored and the meeting brought to an end only when Mrs Burnett, the chairman of the managers, undertook to chair a further meeting at which parents and teachers could discuss their differences in a calmer atmosphere. But the second meeting, held on 9 July, was no more successful than the first. The teachers, badly shaken by the way the 13 June meeting turned out, had finally agreed to attend only after assurances that someone from the ILEA's divisional office would be there and that there would be no personal attacks on individual members of staff. Mrs Walker made a fierce attack on the school. Mrs Burnett allowed a parent to put a question, reasonable enough in the circumstances, about Mr Haddow's teaching methods. This was interpreted by the staff as a personal attack and Mr Haddow walked out, followed by most of the teachers, leaving Mr Ellis, unhappily isolated, to see out the rest of the meeting.

An atmosphere of mutual mistrust had now been generated, which was to prove impossible to dissipate. Along with Mrs Dewhurst, Mrs Gittings had been a frequent and often welcome visitor at the school; now even her visits were regarded with suspicion. Mr Auld made it clear in his report that Mrs Walker must bear a large part of the responsibility for this. After pinning her statement to the staff noticeboard, she talked about it and circulated it to parents, and though, being opposed to strike action, she did not attend the start of the 13 June meeting, she turned up towards the end of it. No formal complaint was laid against her and nobody suggested that her temporary contract should be terminated; it was not until Christmas that she left the school and eventually went back to her previous job at Dulwich College Preparatory School. At the very least, by her actions that summer term, she had encouraged the development of the seige mentality which was to become an increasingly noticeable feature of the teachers' behaviour over the next eighteen months.

Meanwhile the local authority was being brought into the conflict. Donald Rice, the new district inspector, had attended the 9 July meeting; he had also been asked for a report on the school on the intiative of Harvey Hinds, who, as chairman of the schools subcommittee and chief whip of the Labour group on the GLC, was at the time second only to Sir Ashley Bramall in the education committee's political hierarchy. Mr Hinds had been alerted by Anne Page, the Islington member of the ILEA, who had in turn been alerted by questions from Mrs Burnett at a conference for managers about the exact powers of managers when it came to the crunch. Mr Rice's report, in any case fairly anodyne, did not reach Mr Hinds; its only concrete result was an extra grant of £700 for children with special difficulties in the junior school the following term. Of rather more consequence was a meeting of Mrs Burnett, Mrs Gittings and another manager, Valeria Fairweather, with divisional office after the end of term. Much to their surprise, they found Mr Rice flanked by no less than three senior ILEA officers who bluntly told the managers 'to cool it'. They said, among other things, that it was only reasonable to give a new headteacher a full year in office before contemplating any action. This was interpreted by the managers as meaning that Mr Ellis had until Christmas to get his school sorted out, and Mrs Fairweather passed that on to Mr Ellis at the beginning of the September term.

Mrs Fairweather's action destroyed any chance that there might have been that teachers and managers could start off on a better and friendlier footing; staffroom paranoia set in straight away. With the help of divisional office, they even got the managers, at their October meeting, to pass a vote of confidence in the school and its staff and to announce it to all the parents. It was a pretty hollow vote of confidence, though. After those summer holidays the number of children in the school dropped by one quarter. Among those who took their children away from the junior school were Mrs Dewhurst (who, ceasing to be a junior parent, was thereby no longer a manager) and Mrs Gittings. Another manager who clearly had no confidence in the school was Robin Mabey, a local councillor, who came in one day without prior notice and stood silently at the back of a class; the purpose of his visit, he said later, was to check out a rumour that the teachers were using Monopoly to show the children how to undermine capitalism.

On a more serious level, towards the end of that autumn term, Brenda Hart, the very popular head of the infant school, took her complaints to the divisional officer, the direct representative of the education officer in Islington. She had already felt obliged to put the interests of her school before professional solidarity when, back in June, she and her staff had asked the district inspector, Mr Rice, to come and listen to their complaints about the noise, the interruptions and the violence they and the infant children had to put up with from the juniors. To these complaints, Miss Hart now added one of 'reverse racism' – by which she meant that black children were being favoured at the expense of white. Mr Ellis and the junior school staff also took their complaints against the managers higher up. At the end of September, in what Mr Auld regarded as a very important plea for help, they wrote to Mr Hinds at County Hall asking him to receive a deputation from the staff; Mr Hinds turned down their request.

The strain was beginning to tell on everybody. Tempers got shorter, with children as well as with adults. Mr Ellis was frequently away sick – a sure sign, if any more were needed, that all was not well – and his wife complained to the authority about the strain he was under. Mrs Burnett, too, became ill, and resigned for personal reasons as chairman of the managers halfway through the next term.

None of that, however, deterred the staff from putting into practice the teaching organisation they had planned. Two new teachers, both sympathetic to Mr Haddow's ideas, had joined the staff, so that, with the exception of Mrs Chowles at the top end of the school and Mrs McColgan at the bottom, a child-centred, free-choice approach was now the order of the day. Except in the fourth year, what the staff called team-teaching, and Mr Auld co-operative teaching, became the rule: a team of four, for example, under Mr Haddow, looked after the second and third years, using an open-plan approach which meant that the corridor and three classrooms with their doors open were available for the different activities the children were free to choose from. There was also, from the end of November onwards, a plan for a cloakroom to be transformed into a 'sanctuary' where particularly disruptive children could go to have small group therapy sessions with a part-time teacher who was also a student at the Tavistock Institute.

Things did not work out quite as smoothly as the theory suggested, and children were often unsupervised. Teachers were frequently called away for staff meetings. As the year wore on, nearly every time Mr Ellis had an official visitor, Mr Haddow, the mainstay of his team of four, would leave his corridor post and be in there, with the head and his visitor, taking notes. The number of potentially disruptive children was far greater than the Tavistock psychotherapist could possibly cope with. Besides a sanctuary for them, William Tyndale also had, in common with many other schools, a room, referred to cynically by the teachers as a BFR or 'broken furniture room', which was used to store the remains of the desks, chairs, and so on that had fallen victim to the children's rage.

One of the new teachers, David Austin, had responsibility for 'children with special difficulties'. To keep them occupied and interested, he thought up the idea of forming a steel band, and with some difficulty and ingenuity got together the necessary instruments. In one sense, this band was a great success: it did keep a number of children interested, and it turned out to be quite a good band (they played in a primary exhibition at County Hall in the summer term) so that it could be presented as a positive achievement for the school. On the other hand, once they had got their own drums in February, it can hardly have reassured those who thought the school was too noisy and disorderly or those who were worried that, noisy or not, the school was not fulfilling its prime task of teaching 'the basics' – reading, writing and arithmetic.

On that question, Christmas 1974 marked the end of the year's 'honeymoon' which the authority had insisted on according Mr Ellis. Now the managers – or, more accurately, a group of them – took the gloves off. This coincided with the appointment to the managing body of Elisabeth Hoodless, a tough-minded local activist with a reputation for getting things done, and the replacement as chairman of the managers of Mrs Burnett by Brian Tennant. One of the group's first acts was to initiate a meeting with Mr Hinds of Mrs Hoodless, Mrs Fairweather and a couple of other people; neither Mr Tennant nor the other managers were informed of the meeting. As a result of that meeting, Mr Rice was asked to visit the school and report back. His report contained little of substance: a number of things were certainly wrong, but the problems of William Tyndale were basically no different from those of other schools and, left to themselves, the staff would probably be able to cope. The authority's conclusion was that Mr Rice's visit should be followed up by other inspectors who would 'give guidance in specialist areas'. However, no such specialist visit took place until a music inspector went to the school in July, and no further action was taken on the report.

After he had received the report, Mr Hinds met Mrs Hoodless and her friends again. Pressed by them, he made it plain that the authority could not take action unless there was evidence of dissatisfaction within the community: the word 'petition' was mentioned, and that was enough to set Mrs Hoodless, together with an Islington borough councillor, organising the collection of signatures to go under the following text, which was to be sent to the ILEA:

We the undersigned are concerned at the deteriorating quality of education at William Tyndale Junior School and note the rapid decline in the roll at a time when neighbouring schools are full and call upon the ILEA to take urgent action to restore public confidence in this junior school.

The action that Mrs Hoodless had in mind was the merging of the junior and infant schools into a single establishment under the headship of Miss Hart.

That was the beginning of the end. At their May meeting the managers discussed the falling roll and passed a resolution along the same lines as the petition. The staff, who had not heard about the petition until the beginning of the summer term, responded by campaigning round other schools in the area; in June, the North London Teachers' Association passed a resolution designed to discourage other schools from admitting children withdrawn from William Tyndale. Mr Mabey and his fellow ward councillors protested at this in a letter to the *Islington Gazette*. Mr Ellis wrote a final letter to Mr Rice asking, in vain, for help. The staff decided to ban all visits of managers during school hours. This was one way of recognizing the complete breakdown in relations between managers and teachers, but because of the definite, though imprecise, legal implications of such a move, the effect was to unite all the managers, including several who were not at all happy at the way the petition had been handled. At the end of June, the hard-line caucus of managers decided to go to the press and at the beginning of July Mrs Burnett released a statement to *The Times*. The William Tyndale affair was now headlines.

On 2 July, far too late to do any good, Mr Hinds called a meeting of administrators, teachers and managers at County Hall. If it was an attempt to knock everybody's heads together, it failed. The managers called for an inspection by the Department of Education and Science. Mr Hinds, however, hesitated to support such a move, preferring an ILEA inspection. His description of what that would involve led everybody to believe that it could include the role of the managers. The staff, after the week's breathing period, opposed that and asked for an investigation by the Secretary of State for Education and Science under Section 93 of the 1944 Education Act. The authority, however, settled for a formal inquiry, to be preceded by an ILEA inspection. This was all to happen the following term.

When the time came, the teachers, having failed to obtain satisfaction over the terms of the inspection and inquiry, went on strike, against the advice of their union. As a result, the inspection, farcically, took place in a vacuum. Mr Ellis and his followers took twenty-seven children with them and opened a rival school in a chapel hall in Gaskin Street, while the inspectors and, later, temporary teachers kept the original school going. The managers attempted to 'lock out' Mr Ellis and his staff, but they finally obeyed the instructions of both the authority and their union and went back to William Tyndale for a formal inspection in October. By then, however, the school had well and truly fallen apart. It remained to be seen whether anybody, particularly Mr Auld, QC, who headed the inquiry, could put it together again.

2. The Islington Setting

The job description of the post of headteacher of William Tyndale Junior School prepared by the ILEA contained the following passages:

> William Tyndale lies back from Upper Street, Islington, near the Town Hall. The role [the number of children in the school] is approximately 250; present indications are that the numbers may remain steady, though there is a general trend downwards in Islington. . . . The children are from a wide range of backgrounds. Though these are mostly working class and some parents are very poor, there has been an increasing choice of this school by middle-class and professional families from the Canonbury area. The proportion of immigrants (roughly 16 per cent) is low and there are few language problems.

The twin concerns of the ILEA, administrative and educational, were clear enough. In an ideal world, a falling school population should simply have resulted in smaller class sizes but in practice it meant that some resources, both teachers and buildings, had to be redeployed. In May 1972, Mr Hinds, the chairman of the schools subcommittee of the ILEA, said in answer to a question in committee, 'So far as Islington's entitlement to primary teachers is concerned, a fall of over 1,000 pupils from one year's estimates to the next is leading to a reduction of 4·5 full time equivalent teachers'. (This is not a very big reduction, even allowing for the fact that numbers never fall by an exact class size in every school.) If the number of pupils in a school falls below a certain figure, it is considered 'unviable' and closed or amalgamated with another school; in the case of William Tyndale, that number was 80 for the junior school and 80 for the infant school. As it was, with a roll of 217, the new headteacher had quite a margin to play with. Educationally, too, the prospects were good: few immigrants, and so 'few language problems', which make a heavy call on resources, and an increasing number of presumably more highly motivated children from the 'middle-class and professional families'. There was every chance, therefore, so the job description implied, that a new headteacher would be able to maintain a high educational standard in the school and so continue to attract parents from outside its immediate catchment area. The viability of William Tyndale was not expected to be in doubt.

The extent and consequences of the falling school population of Islington were, however, greater than the job description indicated. Nationally, though the total population had continued to rise, since 1964 the birth rate had steadily declined. The population forecasters failed properly to anticipate the decline, so that, since buildings had to be planned well in advance, during the 1960s teachers had been trained and schools built for thousands of schoolchildren of the late 1970s and early 1980s who were turning out not to be there. This combined with a general movement of population out of city centres into the suburbs and the countryside – a movement which had been particularly noticeable in London – to make for smaller and smaller inner city schools.

If London was badly affected by these trends, Islington was worse. The borough's population, which had been declining steadily since its peak of just over 400,000 near the turn of the century, had dropped by a record 23 per cent in the ten years between 1961 and 1971, and was continuing to decline at the rate of 7,000 a year, so that by the middle of 1975 there were thought to be only 175,000 people living in Islington. This decline had more to do with migration than with birth rates; some people were moving into the borough to live, but far more were moving out. Moreover, those moving out were often couples with young families, which was one of the factors that made educational planning very difficult. The ILEA had figures which illustrated this. In the school year 1963/4, nearly twice as many babies were born in the whole of inner London as were born ten years later; in Islington the difference was even greater, two and a half times.

But what really made Islington stand out was the difference in the 'survival' rate. That is not as macabre as it sounds. The survival rate was the term used by educational statisticians to describe the relationship between the number of babies born in an area and the number who turned up in school six years later. Thus, if every baby born in 1970 turned up for school in 1976, the survival rate would have been 100 per cent; if none turned up, it would have been 0 per cent. In 1960, in inner London as a whole, the survival rate was around 70 per cent; in Islington, at that time, it was rather higher – nearer 75 per cent. Fifteen years later, the rate for inner London had dropped a little, to around 66 per cent; in Islington, during that time, it had dropped dramatically to 50 per cent in 1970, and had picked up again slightly to 58 per cent

28

by 1975. Some of those babies died, some were educated in special schools, some in private schools; but by far the biggest proportion just went to live elsewhere.

The ILEA had all the information but, concerned as it was primarily with administration and teaching, it did not appear to have inquired into the reasons for it, and it certainly did not fully appreciate the consequences. According to evidence presented by the ILEA to a meeting of William Tyndale managers, from 1972 to 1975 only William Tyndale, out of five neighbouring schools, was showing a marked drop in the number of pupils – though according to a later check in 1976, of the seven schools within a two-mile radius of William Tyndale only two had anything like their full complement of pupils. But whatever the details, the main result was that parents could now pick and choose in a way that had not been possible before. If they disapproved of what was going on in a school, they could exercise the only real sanction open to them – to take their children away and put them in another school. It happened to William Tyndale; it has happened to other London schools; and it is likely to happen again wherever there are more school places than there are schoolchildren.

The declining population of Islington, then, was an essential part of the William Tyndale saga; indeed, without it, the story might have been very different. The school's falling roll was created by first a few and then a host of parents taking their children away. This in turn became a stick with which the managers beat the headteacher and his staff and the grounds on which they complained to the ILEA and organised petitions within the community. The teachers also felt strongly about it. When in the summer of 1975 they tried, through their union, to put pressure on other schools not to accept children who had been taken away from William Tyndale, they did not see this simply as a move to counteract the managers' attack upon them. There was a real danger that the authority would be forced to close William Tyndale, and they felt most strongly that parents should not be in a position to destroy a school in this way. A lot of Islington headteachers and other teachers who disapproved of what was going on at William Tyndale supported them over this; after all, where might it not end? Accountability to parental consumers was not yet part of a teacher's vocabulary.

The job description was right to emphasise the population trends in Islington, though it was perhaps oversanguine about their effects on William Tyndale. But Laurie Buxton, the district inspector who wrote it shortly before moving to another job as staff inspector for mathematics, gave a rather inadequate account of the educational position. There may have been only a few language problems, but by the time Mr Ellis took up his post more than a third of the school was classified as being in need of remedial classes for reading and writing. The cynic might suggest that that was implicit in the information that the children's backgrounds were 'mostly working class and some of these are very poor', though that would be a poor comment on schools generally. However, the main criticism of that job description must be that it treated children-in-school as quite divorced from children-in-the-home or children-in-the-community; the question was the effect the children could have on the school, rather than how the school could help the children.

Islington's planning department, however, looked at the school rather differently. Over the last few years, it has produced a number of local area studies. One of these, published in October 1974, looked at the area round William Tyndale School. The Wakelin/Halton area, as it was called, took in all the flats surrounding the school, bounded on the outside by Upper Street, Cross Street, Essex Road, Canonbury Road and Canonbury Lane. Three of the five estates were prewar, two of them dating from the 1920s, and altogether they contained around 3,000 people including 700 children of school age. William Tyndale School was described as follows:

> This has separate infant and junior schools with two headmasters. It is also used in the evenings by Highbury Manor adult education institute. The site and facilities are somewhat below standard for the 350 pupils, but the school, which was modernised about 10 years ago, does not rank highly in the ILEA list of priorities. The intake is expected to drop as the Borough population falls, and it is thus anticipated that the school will continue to function with fewer pupils. The school also has a separate nursery class catering for about 50 pupils in two shifts. The playground has recently been equipped with facilities to allow it to play a role outside school hours, but a playleader has not yet been appointed.

The description and the concerns – with the continued existence of William Tyndale as a play and recreation centre out of school hours – were quite different from those of the ILEA job description. The area lacks any amenity of that sort; the nearest parks, Finsbury and Clissold, are literally miles away – even Highbury Fields is on the other side of some of the worst traffic in Islington. In two of the estates, there were signs of acute conflict between young people and other residents because 'there are too few proper recreational facilities to meet the needs of the local children and young people'. Though some of the conflict, the authors thought, could be put down to 'the normal results of unrestrained children's play', there also appeared to be an increase in 'hard-core malicious vandalism'.

But perhaps most interesting, in view of later developments, was the study's summary of the main issues in the area:

> The argument for according a high priority to these estates is, however, based not only on physical condition but on the particular social problems of this area . . . and the lack of social organisation. Unlike other estates the tenants of these blocks seem unable to organise themselves adequately to put forward their views or to influence their own future. . . . A parallel can be drawn between these estates and the problems currently besetting secondary education, with a downward spiral of deprivation being created which becomes harder to break as time goes by. *In our view it is essential that a positive attempt is made to break this downward spiral now with a broad based attack to improve living conditions in these estates. This should be based not only on an improvement in physical conditions, but also in terms of social organisation and management.* (original italics)

So the children who formed the bulk of William Tyndale's intake were frustrated and some of them at least were taking to delinquency, while their parents remained, on the whole, apathetic and unwilling or unable to organise themselves. But the 'downward spiral of deprivation' was by no means confined to this area; it was affecting the whole of Islington.

The borough's popular historical reputation tends to be based on pawnbroking ('pop goes the weasel'), prizefighting, still commemorated in one or two of the inn signs in the remarkable cluster of pubs at the bottom of Upper Street, and the markets, which still survive in Chapel Street and Camden Passage. Part of the sandwich filling between the railway lines running out from King's Cross and Liverpool Street, it boomed in the railway age, tripling in population size between 1851 and 1901. Great private housing estates grew up, such as Mildmay and Scott. But decline set in almost immediately, and became acute from 1930 onwards. The lopsided town hall stands today as a symbol of Islington's change of fortune. Designed in the 1920s, it became a bone of contention between the local Conservative and Labour parties.

Finally, the Conservatives started building it, but not according to the original grandiose plans. Instead of the north wing of the town hall, they erected a block of flats, Tyndale Mansions North, with its much smaller sister, Tyndale Mansions South, on the other side. In the 1970s the council was looking for more office space – but that was to accommodate an expansion of bureaucracy, not population.

The population, though falling, was always to some extent renewing itself. Islington had long been a place where Jews came on their way out of the East End, a sort of staging post on the way up to Golders Green or Hampstead. More recently, families of West Indian and, even more, Turkish or Cypriot origins came to settle there. Most of them ended up in the Finsbury area, to the north of the borough, so that there were comparatively few in St Mary's ward, where William Tyndale was located. Those that had settled there, though, tended to show the same symptoms of social deprivation and psychological disturbance that were often associated with areas of high concentration of immigrant families. Of the three trouble-making boys who were most often discussed in William Tyndale's staffroom, two were West Indian in origin and one Turkish.

The psychological disturbances – bible-punching fathers, single-parent families – they may have brought with them; the social deprivation, they found on arrival in Islington. The 1971 census showed that, in terms of overcrowded housing, the sharing of basic amenities such as baths and toilets, and male unemployment, in the whole of Great Britain only Glasgow was a worse place than Islington to live. Interestingly, Islington's first reaction in the postwar years, when it had been dominated by a traditional Labour council, had been the same as Glasgow's: a massive programme of rehousing through demolition and construction. That proved hideously expensive and did not solve all the problems. More recently, the council began to turn away from building new dwellings to a policy of renovating existing houses and flats. This was partly done by the council itself, partly by offering generous improvement grants to those who would do it themselves. This happened to coincide with the time when young middle-class and professional families began to move into Islington, buying up run-down low-cost housing in areas previously considered socially unacceptable and turning them into ideal Habitat or Heal's homes.

This had occurred in other areas of London, such as Fulham, to a much greater extent than in Islington but, perhaps because of its nearness to Fleet Street and the City, Islington seemed to have attracted a particular type of socially aware, politically active middle-class citizen, who as managers and parents were to play perhaps a disproportionately large role in the William Tyndale conflict. They began, so to speak, by encircling the school in enclaves which were, or became, conservation areas: Barnsbury to the west, Waterloo Terrace and Cross Street to the south, Canonbury to the east and Highbury to the north. The only gap in the ring was to the north-west, up the Holloway Road, where there was a job centre with the highest unemployment in the whole of London.

By their presence, these people drew attention to problems which might otherwise have remained dormant in the council's files. On others, such as traffic in Barnsbury or the threatened closure of a secondary school, they formed action groups themselves. Again, by their very existence, they highlighted the central dilemma for the growing numbers of social workers in Islington: should they be agents of change or agents of control? On occasion, in the area where these people had settled, they joined with social workers in trying to promote change by supporting strikes or other forms of direct action. They also moved into politics – Labour politics, mainly, because Labour was the party of government in Islington. For nearly forty years, with a brief interlude of Conservative rule from 1968 to 1971, the council had been dominated by a caucus of men with strong trade union connections – the sort of people for whom, often, revolution was a dirty word, order came before change and the helpless were thought of as the feckless. By 1972 and 1973 the newcomers had ousted the old guard from most of the key positions; names that were to recur during the saga of William Tyndale – the Mabeys of Waterloo Terrace, the Fairweathers of Battishill Street, the Hoodlesses of Cross Street – could be found as vice-chairman of the policy committee, chairman of town planning and development, chairman of social services, and so on. While the husbands made hay in the town hall, the wives (and sometimes the husbands as well) provided some new, more active blood in the managing and governing bodies of schools.

At the same time, the council became noticeably more concerned with participation. It took pains to tell its electorate what the problems were and ask it what it wanted done about them. Education was seen as one of those problems. In 1975 the council, prior to drawing up an Islington Borough Plan, published a newsletter, which set out in eight pages 'what is wrong with Islington' and included a questionnaire designed to test people's attitudes to priorities between and within different services, such as housing, social services, transport, education, and so on. The council also carried out a household interview survey, and held a series of public meetings.

The newsletter began by putting the problem as seen by the council in a nutshell: 'Bad housing, poor surroundings, old school buildings, fewer jobs, low wages all encourage people to leave.' Most of those who answered the questionnaire thought that the two services on which it was most important to spend more money were housing and education. On the whole they did not have a very high opinon of education in Islington: nearly three-quarters of those who complained of the general lack of discipline and thought the schools were 'bad' or 'disgusting' turned out not to have children at school (though that is not necessarily a reason for ignoring their views). Overall, from the whole exercise, the council drew the following conclusions on education:

> In the field of education the main concern was with the need for the Council to urge the ILEA *to raise educational standards in the borough* though there was nowhere a definition of what raised standards would constitute [*sic*]. It was asserted that in part this could be done by resisting the pressure to close schools as roles [*sic*] fall and instead reducing class sizes. The view was expressed that responsibility for educational standards did not lie solely with the ILEA. It was asserted that there was a direct relationship between *low educational attainment and poor housing conditions*. The resolution of this is seen to lie in part with Islington Council.

The difficulty was that Islington did not control its own schools. As the newsletter put it: 'Education is an important part of the life of a community, and must play a role in the Islington Plan. Islington collects £15,500,000 from you as ratepayers – 34p in every £1 you pay – and hands it over to the Inner London Education Authority, which is in charge of education in Islington.'

The ILEA was also in charge of education in the eleven other inner London boroughs, which the ILEA had compressed into ten divisions. It was this which made the administration of education in London different from that anywhere else in the country. Elsewhere, the education authority was one department of a local authority along with others, such as social services, housing, environment, and so on. Local government reorganisation, which came into effect in 1974, created three types of local authority on two different levels. The result was that some local authorities responsible for education also had responsibility for, say, housing while others did not. But the elected members of education committees were also members of full councils and as such had a say in the administration of other services which had links, directly or indirectly, with education. Officers, too, could walk down the corridor, or at worst across the street, to consult their colleagues whenever there was an overlap or conflict of interest.

That was not true of London. The ILEA was an *ad hoc* education committee of the GLC and, though manned by it, serviced by it and financed by it, remained in theory and in practice largely independent of it. Its task was to administer the education service for the inner London boroughs which ran a good many of their other services themselves. As Islington pointed out in its newsletter, these had to collect the rates, bear the main thrust of ratepayer dissatisfaction, and then send a third of them on to the GLC at County Hall to pay the ILEA's costs. Between them, the local electors in the inner London boroughs elected thirty-five members of the GLC; these, plus a representative from each borough council, sat on the ILEA's education committee (which also had seventeen co-opted members). The leader and deputy leader of the ILEA were generally appointed from among the members of the ruling party on the GLC. Those GLC members, together with the borough representatives, were the only institutional link between the boroughs and the ILEA, though some contact was also maintained through Labour and Conservative party groups. But there was no provision for any contact between ILEA and borough officers.

The ILEA, therefore, was an isolated and hybrid animal with, understandably perhaps, a rather narrow interpretation of the services it was in business to provide. Being a centralised bureaucracy, with the job of resisting the various centrifugal forces pulling at it, the authority acquired a reputation for taking decisions in a centralised, bureaucratic manner. It had few friends and many enemies, among which were the boroughs of Islington and Kensington and Chelsea. In 1975 both of these councils set up education advisory committees. Clearly, such committees could not usurp any of the functions of the ILEA, but they served to underline the conviction of those councils that the elected authority closest to the ratepayer had, at the very least, a right to express a considered view on education matters within its own boundaries for which it was paying.

The feeling that something should be done about the over-centralisation of the ILEA was not confined to Islington and

Kensington borough councillors. Soon after coming to the ILEA as deputy education officer in 1972, Peter Newsam (who was appointed to succeed Eric Briault on his retirement as education officer in January 1977) put forward a proposal for a degree of administrative devolution. Under this plan, the ten divisional officers, whose function at the time was mainly administrative and co-ordinating, would have become divisional education officers with the same responsibilities in their separate divisions as the education officer had for the whole of the ILEA. Mr Newsam found some support for his proposal among Labour members, but it foundered largely on opposition from the GLC staff association. A similar proposal from a Labour group working party, but based on four regions rather than ten divisions, was also shelved. More recently, the Conservatives have also looked into the question. In 1975, Geoffrey Finsberg, MP for Hampstead, headed a policy working party on London; he asked Ian Clarke, a Conservative member of the ILEA, to look at the education authority, and Mr Clarke concluded that it was in fact feasible administratively and politically to break up the ILEA and hand responsibility for education back to the inner London boroughs. But by the time Mr Auld presented his report the only change that had taken place was a slight devolution of the education officer's responsibilities to the senior assistant education officers at County Hall.

In the face of all that pressure going back several years, it did not make much sense to say, as the William Tyndale teachers frequently maintained, that the managers' attacks on their school were all part of a plot to show up the ILEA's incompetence and boost the importance of the Islington educational advisory committee. There were some Labour members in Islington who would have liked to see the ILEA broken up, but most would have been happy with some form of devolution. Like Mrs Page, the Islington borough council representative on the ILEA, they were most distressed at what was happening to the school and most angry about the ILEA's role in it, but there were no grounds for any suggestion that any of them sought to aggravate the position at the school for political ends. The advisory committee, for example, was most careful not to put William Tyndale on to its agenda until the inquiry was well under way. Undoubtedly though, in this as in so many areas, the events of William Tyndale highlighted issues and conflicts that had tended to remain dormant, at least as far as the general public was concerned.

We now turn to look at what was actually going on in the school.

3. The Heart of the Matter

The sound of glass being smashed on the playground, a young voice wildly chanting, 'Black is power, White is flour'. A boy of West Indian parentage, whom we shall call Homer Eliot, the terror of William Tyndale, was at it again. Up on the roof of the lavatories, which abut on to the main school building, dancing, screaming, he hurled down the milk bottles and refused to budge. Eventually he allowed himself to be pursuaded by Mr Haddow – often the only person he would allow himself to be persuaded by – and came down. But the violence and the abuse continued. In the end, Mr Haddow and Mr Austin together had to frogmarch him, while he screamed racial insults at them, all the way up Upper Street to his home and the thrashing his teachers knew he would get from his father.

That particular incident happened in 1975, when conflicts among the staff and between the teachers and the managers were already tearing the school apart. It was typical in one sense at least: repeated in one form or another countless times, that sort of noisy, violent disruption provoked Miss Hart, the headteacher of the infant school, into going to the divisional office of the ILEA to complain about her colleagues in the junior school. But the incident also illustrates the central question at the heart of the William Tyndale dispute: what to do with children like Homer Eliot who obstinately refuse to accept any limitation upon the free expression of their uncontrolled will. Do you take the view that there is more joy in Heaven over one sinner that repenteth than over ninety and nine just men, and do all you can to keep him in school by bending the rules and finding ways of channelling his furious energy into something – anything – less destructive? Or do you, for the sake of the majority of the children and the teachers' sanity, refuse to have him in the school at all?

For Miss Hart, the answer had been straightforward: Homer Eliot had been one of her pupils in the infant school, and she had set in motion the referral process. This was a lengthy business which could lead, via interviews with educational psychologists, and so on, to a place in a school for maladjusted children. However, there were not enough such places for all the children referred in this way, and so many of them either stayed where they were or ended up in special schools for the 'educationally subnormal'.

So Homer Eliot was still at William Tyndale when he came of age to go up into the junior school. By 1974/5 he was probably the most disruptive influence in the school, but he was still there, very intelligent but totally illiterate. Unlike the infant school ones, though, his junior school teachers wanted to keep him. Their reasoning, as Mr Austin put it to us, was that the one sure way of creating a delinquent at the age of 18 was to reject him at school and so brand him indelibly as a social outcast. If only they could keep him in school, they argued, there was still a faint chance that he might latch on to something which might hold his interest long enough for him to become amenable to learning at least a few basic skills. It was a tenable position; if it meant that other children suffered as a result of people like Homer Eliot remaining in the school, then the teachers might have justified their approach, if they had felt so inclined, by reference to the Christian ethic and the parable of the lost sheep.

In fact, in Homer Eliot's case, the approach could be said to have worked, up to a point at least. The boy and his family were well known to the various social services and Mr Ellis and Mr Austin attended a case conference about him. As Mr Austin remembered it, there were about forty people there: social workers, educational welfare officers, health visitors, probation officers, and so on. The two representatives of his school heard that the boy had been recommended for a place in a special school as soon as one became available. They argued to be allowed to keep him at William Tyndale, assuring the conference that they would be able to give Homer Eliot something he would really like – the chance to play in an all-steel band. And that is how they obtained the authorisation to spend ILEA money on equipping William Tyndale with the necessary instruments. For the rest of the year Homer Eliot stayed at school and practised with the band; the following year, however, when temporary staff took over the running of the school, one teacher had to be assigned to look after him virtually full-time.

That story illustrates in a small way how the disagreements in the William Tyndale staffroom were not fundamentally about teaching methods as such. Though it came to be seen as a dispute between the progressives and the traditionalists, and though the debate was largely conducted along those lines with attitudes hardening all the while, teaching methods were merely a convenient vehicle through which different and deeper conflicts about school and society were thrashed out. Miss Hart, for example, who once took a diametrically opposed line to Mr Ellis over Homer Eliot, could not have been accused of being anti-progressive by her worst enemies. As a young headteacher, she had taken over what she saw as a traditionally run infant school back in 1967. Her first move was to abolish rote learning and to give the children more freedom; as Mr Ellis was to do, she dismantled the ordered rows of desks and reorganised classes into small informal groups which overflowed out of the classrooms into the corridors. At first this brought signs of some of the trouble Mr Ellis was later to run into: children wandering into other classes and disrupting them, and anxious parents demanding explanations. But because Miss Hart was not prepared to let the disruptive few imperil the success of her innovations, she imposed strict limits on where children could and could not go and for those who were seen as having behavioural problems she arranged therapy sessions away from the main part of the school, first in a storeroom and later in a separate building. And for the really difficult cases, like Homer Eliot, she put in motion the referral procedure.

So, whereas the junior school staff were prepared to put at risk all that they were trying to do in the school for the sake of the minority of children who were otherwise destined to form the very bottom of the social heap, Miss Hart was definitely not. She was even prepared to put the preservation of her infant school in the form she wanted before professional solidarity; twice in the first year of Mr Ellis's headship, she complained to ILEA inspectors about the way in which the junior school children were being allowed to make her task impossible. But the way the junior school staff responded was revealing. They attacked her claim that what she was doing was 'progressive'. 'Pretty, pretty' sort of stuff, they said, and referred scathingly to all the children's work with which the infant school walls, in marked contrast to the junior's, were decorated; all cleverly designed to impress the middle-class parents, but not, they sneered, truly progressive.

Few people care to admit that as time goes on things can get worse, so 'progressive' is good, and the William Tyndale teachers, who firmly believed that what they were doing was progressive, arrogated to themselves that label. They arrogated it to themselves, moreover, for everything they were doing in the school, so that anybody who attacked even a tiny part of what they were doing laid himself or herself open to the charge of being anti-progressive. The technique has commonly been used by priests and politicians through the ages. It was used against Miss Hart and, to much greater effect because the cap fitted rather better, against

Mrs Walker. But there is some reason for believing that even in Mrs Walker's case the real point at issue was not progressive education as such, but the emphasis put on those whom a teacher in another school once described as 'my future criminals'.

That particular teacher was working in a London secondary school, and he used to find that his only chance of talking to his future criminals in school hours was to go and join them in the cafe across the street. Truancy was not quite such a serious problem in primary schools, even in the worst inner city areas, but the hard-core difficult cases at William Tyndale would not come to school and stay there simply because their teachers had decided not to try and get them into special schools for maladjusted children. They had to be bribed, so to speak, by being allowed to do almost exactly what they wanted to do. The 'free choice' teaching methods which Mr Haddow introduced for his fourth-year class during Mr Ellis's first term were extended to all activities throughout the school. No place in the school was put out of bounds to them, not even the staff commonroom and lavatories. They were allowed to eat sweets whenever they wanted, wherever they wanted. To all intents and purposes, there were no rules at all. As Mrs Walker put it in the first of her various papers to be made public:

> Children are being <u>seduced</u> to behave in ways which are detrimental to them, both in their progress in learning anything and in producing anti-social behaviour. They are growing up ignorant, selfish, rude (to the extent that even those manners they learn at home are being eroded) lazy, effete. In order to get them to do any work or make any effort you have to bribe them, cajole, persuade, threaten and spend endless TIME because of the unreasonableness and immaturity in which they are locked, so that the drain on adult energy and morale is out of all proportion to what is achieved. (original underlining and capitals)

Something, though, was achieved none the less. Writing specifically of the co-operative teaching scheme introduced and led by Mr Haddow in the autumn term 1974, Mr Auld emphasised that one of its successes was 'to provide a stimulus for, and give confidence to, many of the children in the group who were of below average ability and/or who were disturbed children. For some of these children the new regime did begin to produce a change for the better both in their attitude to learning and in their general behaviour.' Because of this and of the general atmosphere in the school, some highly disturbed children came regularly to school, who would not otherwise have done so. In Mr Ellis's and Mr Haddow's terms, that would certainly have counted as a success.

The cost of that success, however, was an almost deliberate lack of order and structure throughout the school, and that is what Mrs Walker objected to most strongly. Her final paper, the one which came to be known as the Black Paper, and which she distributed to everybody at the parents'/teachers' meeting in July, was called 'A Criticism of the "Free Choice" Method of Education Based on Total Children's Rights as at William Tyndale Junior School'. She was not of the 'spare the rod and spoil the child' school of thought, which would have children marching about in columns of two and responding to blows of a whistle, and indeed wrote in the paper quoted earlier, 'Since time immemorial people of good sense have surely understood that making a child happier, more self-confident, more interested and contented, helps it to progress in learning as well'. But in her eyes that did not entail staff regularly turning up late, the endless discussions after assembly every morning about what each teacher was going to do that day, the daily effort that went into persuading at least some of the children to do something some of the time, and all the other signs, documented by Mr Auld in his report, that the teachers were just not in control of what they were doing.

For Mrs Walker, structure was important for the children; it was also, one suspects, important for herself. The fierce, dogmatic way she reacted to those interminable staffroom discussions which ranged over everything except how the school was going to educate the children; her determination to bring the issue out into the open; her campaign – described by Mr Auld as 'disgraceful' – among parents and politicians against the staff in general and Mr Ellis in particular; and the growing intemperance of her language and actions; all these suggest that the issue went beyond a matter of principle. Up to the age of 11, she had been educated at convent schools abroad and at a high school; she was then sent to a progressive boarding school run by a friend of A. S. Neill, the legendary headmaster of Summerhill. At 18 she had joined, for a short time, the Communist Party.

From convent to communism is a common enough experience in Catholic countries for those who revolt against a certain kind of authoritarian structure, but cannot do without one of some sort. And though she said she was 'ecstatically happy' at her progressive school, she also reproached it strongly with not equipping its pupils to get to university. Of all those who gave evidence to the inquiry on William Tyndale, Mrs Walker was perhaps the most insistent on the duty of the school to equip its children for the next stage of education – in this case, the secondary school. This is not to belittle the force of Mrs Walker's criticisms; it is merely to emphasise that they were less concerned with whether the children sat in rows and learnt their tables by rote or played with sand and water than with the lack of structure in the classroom, the staffroom and the playground. From that point of view, there were some revealing questions in the paper she circulated for parental discussion during that first summer term:

Are we creating an environment in this school in which children
— are encouraged to learn?
— find it easy to concentrate on learning?
— are helped to discover *how* to learn?
— find maximum satisfaction in doing a job well, achieving a standard?

OR

Are we creating an environment in which children
— are unable to settle down to learning easily?
— find it difficult to concentrate and work quietly?
— become bored?
— are confused as to what is expected of them?
— find minimum satisfaction in learning or trying to do so?
— are not motivated to do a job well?
— find too many opportunities to muck about?
— are motivated to play and develop anti-work attitudes?
— are not encouraged to think logically – but to act emotionally and unreasonably?
— are not helped to organise themselves, their activities, their thinking?
— are not helped to develop self-discipline?
— are allowed to become self-indulgent, inconsiderate, rude?
— are tacitly permitted to develop bad habits of all kinds, in manners, attitudes, language (fuck and shit are heard more often than any other words all day long), laziness, slapdash work (when they do any), etc. etc.?

The William Tyndale teachers, having decided to keep those children whom most schools reject, found they could only do so by abandoning most of the rules and regulations which generally govern the conduct of staff and pupils. In this sense, the issues raised by William Tyndale were more commonly found in secondary schools than in primary ones. Such issues concerned most often those children who, rightly or wrongly, felt they had nothing to work for in school, and that school had little to offer them. In secondary schools, this centred on exams and qualifications: the division was between those who stood a chance of obtaining even some minimal ones and those who did not. From sixth-form teachers, who all too often saw their job as being to select and prepare the brighter children for universities, down to the bottom of the school, teachers' attitudes were too frequently conditioned by exam results of one sort or another.

The crux here was the indirect stranglehold which the universities maintained upon the examination system. Some attempts had been made to break this, partly by removing sixth forms altogether from secondary schools, and partly by trying to introduce alternative exams. But the basic question remained: what to do with those for whom the school appeared to offer nothing and who reacted all too often by delinquency, on or off the school premises? One answer which was more relevant, perhaps, in the context of William Tyndale, was put forward by those schools which had tried to function outside the mainstream pattern – Dartington and A. S. Neill's Summerhill, for example, in the private sector, and Michael Duane's Risinghall in Islington or R. F. Mackenzie's Summerhill Academy in Aberdeen in the public sector. The private sector ones, catering mainly for children whose background marked them out as probable survivors in any system, had flourished, though not always in quite their pristine form. The state ones had been crushed: Risinghill was closed by what was then the London County Council in 1965, and Mr Mackenzie was removed in 1974 as headmaster from Summerhill Academy. Nevertheless, partly as a result of their examples, more and more secondary school headmasters could be heard to say, 'We want some other criteria than exam results, whether A level, O level or CSE, for the success of our schools to be measured by'. And they talked about things that had on the face of it nothing to do with education – employment rates of children from their schools, delinquency rates, truancy rates, and so on.

In secondary schools, in fact, an increasingly large number of children were voting, one way or another, with their feet. In primary schools, this was never thought to be a problem in the same way: children still had a lot of schooling before them and there were no exams – particularly after the 11-plus had virtually disappeared – to divide children into sheep and goats, either in their own or their teachers' eyes. And the 'difficult' ones that did have severe 'behaviour' problems could usually be contained in one way or another – if necessary, by shunting them out of the school.

The events of William Tyndale, however, had brought to light the existence in some primary schools of a group of basically unteachable children who had generally been assumed to exist only in secondary schools. In most schools where they existed, such children, disturbed and disrupting, would have come at the bottom of any list of priorities. Mr Ellis and his colleagues put them at the top of theirs, even if that entailed most of the other children having to adapt to a completely different sort of school from the one they and their parents were used to. In those circumstances, arguments that started about organisation – the way a school is run – would quickly become arguments about curriculum – what is taught in the school. In a statement to the inquiry, signed by their lawyer, Mr Ellis and his colleagues said: 'Within the framework of catering for each child's individual needs and abilities at any specific time (as far as is possible) it is the school's policy that every child should leave the school literate and numerate.'

But that did not answer the sort of arguments put forward by Mrs Walker to the effect that total children's rights meant that there was so much chaos that neither the disturbed group of children nor the others were able to learn anything. Mr Ellis, who could easily be provoked into 'throwaway' remarks which he must have regretted later, might well have replied that even if the children were disturbed they had just as much right to be in school as anybody else; that if they were disturbed it was not their fault, but that of their home environment or their own psychological make-up; and learning to read was not all that important anyway, because it was perfectly possible to be a highly successful, but illiterate, scrap-metal merchant. None of that was likely to appeal to any but a very few committed left-wing parents, and it was not surprising that, with Mrs Walker taking up the cudgels on behalf of those whom Mr Ellis had described as 'pushy, working-class parents', the battlelines immediately became drawn along traditionalist versus progressive lines.

Though the William Tyndale debate was not, primarily, about teaching methods, curriculum and organisation were nevertheless linked. In secondary schools, it was easy to see how the link worked. Curriculum refers to what is taught in schools; that was largely dictated by the exam system; that in turn was heavily influenced by the universities, who relied on secondary schools to select their students for them; which was one of the principal reasons why schools spent much more money and devoted far more teacher-hours to sixth-form pupils than to anybody else. In America, there was another link. Worried about rising unemployment among school-leavers, the Americans decided to try and keep students in high school for as long as possible. That was impossible unless what was taught in the schools was made attractive to those whose natural inclination would have been to leave as early as possible, jobs or no jobs. That, very crudely, is why standards in American high schools were commonly reckoned to be so much lower than our own; they were no longer teaching the same sorts of things to the same sorts of students.

In primary schools, where, as we have seen, there were no longer any exams or attainment tests, the connection was not so obvious. But there clearly is a link between the goals of a school, the way it is run, the teaching methods that are used, and the content of what is taught. A lot depends on the way it is presented to both teachers and parents. We shall be looking at that, and at some of the ways different approaches could work out in practice, in the next chapter.

4. Some Outside Influences

A dozen mothers and one father are sitting round the front room of a small council house complaining about the teaching in the local school. One mother is comparing the maths report of her two daughters, one of them at the school, the other in the partially hearing unit of another school. The first one, unsigned by the class teacher and uninitialled by the headteacher, is part of a 500-word discursive essay on the attitude of Tania (not her real name) to life and work:

> Tania is now aware of what is expected from her in mathematics. She comes up with some marvelous suggestions involving real maths work – sometimes she struggles to carry it through but other times she simply isn't prepared for the effort required. Perhaps she lacks trust in me to help her, because she becomes quite unreceptive to my questions and guidance, feeling that she should not need to make an effort to build new knowledge herself; but rather that I should simply tell her what to do – some magic formula! There are signs that she is now seeing maths, like spelling, as being a logical reasoning process rather than a set of rules to be learnt by heart. She is capable of accurate computation in her work and often gets excited when she realises that her idea – her kite for example – is producing real mathematical problems to be solved.

In the case of the other girl, Julia (again not her real name), the report, signed and countersigned, is divided up into subject headings. Under arithmetic, her teacher has written: 'Julia's mechanical maths have improved, but she has difficulty understanding maths problems. This is because she doesn't always read with understanding. If Julia was able to learn all her tables by memory, this would help her.' The first report gave the mother no clue as to what, if anything, was holding Tania back in maths and what, if anything, she could do to help. The second, however, set it all out succinctly in the same language in which her reports were couched when she was a child. At the school from which the first report came, the one about which they were all complaining, there was no evidence which the parents could see that the teachers were actually teaching the children anything at all. As another mother, who clearly lacked a sense of the ridiculous, put it: 'They don't even teach them what day it is. My girl gets up on Saturdays as if she was going to school.'

The school that was coming under fire was not William Tyndale, but an attractive school in a modern estate in south-west London. As with William Tyndale, a popular headteacher with a progressive image had attracted a lot of middle-class children from outside the immediate catchment area, but a new headteacher had been unable to maintain the image; the middle-class parents had withdrawn their children, and the estate parents were in an uproar. Untutored in the ways of pressure groups (they got up a petition and sent it off to County Hall but did not keep a copy of it) and unfamiliar with the way a school is run (they did not even know that there was such an animal as a parent manager – a manager elected by parents), they did not end by bringing the whole edifice down about their ears. There was no evidence of deprivation in the estate; quite the contrary. These parents simply wanted their children to be taught the same things in the same way that they had been taught as children – they all claimed to have enjoyed sitting in rows reciting their tables. Some of them felt they owed everything to their school, and expected today's teachers to do as much for their children – even to the point, as with the mother who was concerned about which day it was, of teaching them things that schools have come to assume are normally the responsibility of the home.

If the teachers – or some of the William Tyndale staff – had been at that meeting, they might have answered along the following lines:

'Yes, it is quite true, you were taught effectively to read, write and count in ways we would now regard as traditional – that is to say, you were sat in disciplined rows and made to learn by heart. But along with the three "Rs" you also learnt a whole lot of other things, like order. And we don't just mean order in the sense of calm and discipline, but order in the sense of ranking; it mattered who came first, who was top and who was bottom. You were taught the importance of being aggressively competitive; individual effort was what mattered. Teamwork was left to the sportsground – if you were lucky enough to have access to one.

'That is what people nowadays call the "hidden curri-

48

culum", the messages that come across as much from the way something is taught as from what is taught. And that is what we are trying to change today. For look at it this way. You got out from the bottom of the heap, not just by being able to do your sums, but through being aware how vital it was to be able to do them better than your neighbour. But by definition that means there were some – many – who got left behind. You can't all be first. The shape of the heap hasn't changed, just because you got off the bottom, even if the whole heap has moved up a notch or two since you were at school. So what about those who stayed at the bottom then, and those who are at the bottom today?

'Well, we believe that the one thing a child needs, particularly one from the bottom of the heap, is confidence. If he finds difficulty in reading, then let him do something else. Let him first acquire the confidence that comes from being allowed to do something that he himself has elected to do. If, into the bargain, it turns out that he does whatever it is well, then with that extra confidence a whole lot more becomes possible. We believe that if you give the children, all children and not just the average and above-average ones, the opportunity to acquire that sort of confidence, then they will come naturally to the "basics" and the other more academic activities. And we also believe that they will be happier and more useful citizens if they do this not by learning to compete with one another but by working together in small groups.'

Nobody put it to us quite like that, but that is the sort of thing a radical progressive teacher might have said. It is not in itself a political position, though it clearly has political implications; it could be argued that it is little more than an egalitarian, as distinct from an elitist, interpretation of the 'equal opportunity for all' position. On the other hand, the statement itself is extremely elitist, not to say arrogant. Behind the bland and persuasive logic, the assumptions have not changed from one generation to another: like some medieval priest, the teacher is still wanting the parents to commit their children unreservedly to him, just as they were committed to their teachers by their parents – and on the same grounds, that is, 'teacher knows best'. No allowance is made for any diversity of views among the parents, nor even for any expression of any views which might be allowed to influence the teachers. Yesterday's teachers were looking for stability, today's for change; but that is the only difference. The goals may have changed, but the means have remained the same.

There is no reason to suppose that any of the William Tyndale teachers would have accepted that statement as it stands, but if it approximates at all to what they were trying to do, then it is not surprising that neither Mr Ellis nor Mr Haddow nor anybody else spelled it out quite so clearly – or quite so crudely – at the inquiry. There is less excuse, though, for not having tried to put it – or something like it – across to the parents, and Mr Auld, in his report, rightly censured Mr Ellis on this point. When Mr Ellis finally, in response to a request from the managers, put forward in the autumn of 1974 a 'statement of aims', it consisted simply of a few short, unhelpful and platitudinous generalities. It may be that he and his staff were unable to work out anything better; it may be that they felt that anything else would have been counter-productive – and by that stage they were probably right. However that may be, the result was that nobody, at any stage, was given any clear, coherent idea of what they were trying to do. We have tried to piece this together, partly from a look at the educational 'baggage' which three of the most influential of the staff, Mr Ellis, Mr Haddow and Mr Austin, brought with them to the school – that is to say, an amalgam of what they had been taught and what they had already done. We shall say something about Mr Ellis's introduction of team-teaching at Charles Lamb School and the course he took at the London Institute of Education; some of the influences to which Mr Haddow had been exposed at Furzedown College of Education; and John Milton School, where Mr Austin taught for four years before joining William Tyndale.

Much of this, of course, was in the mainstream of educational theorising which has long tended to be considerably more pro-gressive than educational practice. As far back as the First World War, people like Susan Isaacs and Homer Lane were running junior schools along anti-authoritarian lines. They were catering, however, only for marginal groups of children. Miss Isaac's school, Malting House, was mainly for children (aged 2 to 10) of Cambridge academics; Mr Lane's school was for delinquent children from infants to 18 years old. After the war, under the influence of the works of Froebel and Piaget and the liberal ideas of inspectors and teachers, who had seen war service, the move-ment spread. It received its public accolade with the publication in 1967 of the Plowden Report, the work of the teachers' advisory council on education which had been set up three years earlier under the chairmanship of Lady Plowden to advise on 'primary education in all its aspects and the transition to secondary education'. Apart from its many recommendations on educational priority areas, smaller classes, greater resources, and so on, the report consecrated the move away from chalk and talk. A cynic might say that it set the seal of establishment approval on the transference from the home to the school, and from the children of prosperous homes to those from the most deprived ones, of the tolerant, liberal, postwar middle-class way of bringing up children: they were there to be listened to as well as to be talked to; and they could be fun. The report was not concerned, to any important extent, with monitoring the effectiveness of the various teaching methods it passed in review; nor was it concerned with the creation of a fairer and juster society.

Those last two points are important. A number of progressive educationalists saw the report as something of a let-down after all the evidence they had poured into it, partly because it was not concerned with social change. That does not mean, either, that the educationists were revolutionaries; it is simply that the 1960s were the heyday of those throughout the world who saw education as a means of bringing about social change. But the 500-page report in fact did far more for progressive education than was thought likely by the educationists at the time, simply because it covered all the ground. Since then, and it is important to bear this in mind in what follows, there has scarcely been a pedagogical or organisational innovation in primary schools that could not be justified in some way or other by reference to Plowden. On the other hand, and of almost as much consequence for what happened at William Tyndale, the Plowden Report, besides providing the progressive movement with its accolade, may also have marked its zenith. Since then, outside the teaching profession and even to some extent inside it, there has been evident a much greater degree of scepticism about both the aims and the methods of much progressive education. To a large extent, this is healthy: the so-called 'Black Papers' on education, which first began to appear under the names of Rhodes Boyson, Brian Cox and others in 1969 (only two years after Plowden), represent only the backlash fringe.

Mr Ellis

Mr Ellis did not originally train to be a teacher. He got a degree from King's College, London, in 1960, and spent a couple of years in a school in Brittany before settling down to teaching in London. As soon as he was appointed deputy head of Charles Lamb Junior School in 1968 he enrolled for a three-year part-time diploma course in primary education at the Institute of Education,

51

London University. Apart from a six-day primary school management course run by the authority in the spring of 1973, that was all the teacher training Mr Ellis had when he came to William Tyndale.

The diploma course was run by Ken Watts, who saw it as a useful link in a two-way information flow. As all his students were required to have been practising teachers for at least three years, and he based the course on what they were actually doing in their schools and classrooms, it enabled the members of the Institute and himself to keep in touch with what at least some teachers were up to. It also served as a link by which some of the ideas emanating from the Institute could filter back to the front-line teacher. The Institute provided a home for a number of well-known educational theorists, such as Professors Basil Bernstein and Harold Rosen, whose ideas would certainly have horrified the parents we met at the beginning of the chapter if they had heard or understood half of them.

At Charles Lamb, an Islington school built in 1870 – even before William Tyndale – Mr Ellis was responsible for setting up and running a team of five teachers looking after 135 children. This involved putting into practice some ideas which are conceptually very simple – such as the integrated day and the 'open' school – though they tend to get hidden in the morass of educational jargon and definitions. What the pundits say is, 'the minimum concept of the integrated day is that of a school day so organised that there are no, or very few, uniform and formalised breaks in the activities of learning and teaching, but rather a variety of such activities going on simultaneously, and changing very much at the choice of the individual child, or perhaps the group' (R. F. Dearden, *The Integrated Day in Theory and Practice*, Ward Lock Educational, 1971). That can cover a multitude of sins, from simply abandoning fixed periods in the classroom to rather bigger changes based on the following premise: it will be easier to keep children's interest and give them individual attention if teachers and pupils are not confined to predetermined classrooms or predetermined class hours; they must be free to move between rooms/areas and subjects/activities as and when it seems appropriate either to the children or to the teacher. It is comparatively easy to put such a scheme into practice in a single-floor, open plan school built for the purpose. One such is Prior Weston School, in The Barbican just to the south-east of Islington, where Henry Pluckrose, building up slowly from only a handful of pupils, had been able to create along those lines a model school which attracted middle-class children not merely from neighbouring Islington but from some way south of the river as well.

It is much more difficult to do it, though, in schools such as William Tyndale and Charles Lamb, designed with traditional classrooms and corridors. Partly, perhaps, because he was able to discuss the problems as he went along in the course sessions, Mr Ellis did it extremely well. The Institute made a video recording of his work and he was highly commended by his headteacher. Curiously, though, he did not make much of this in his application for the headship of William Tyndale; in the 200 words allowed on the form for a 'concise general statement', Mr Ellis had only this to say of his team-teaching at Charles Lamb: 'In the past, as team leader and acting head, I have been concerned with the co-ordination of teaching activities in a situation wider than that of the normal classroom.' His district inspector at the time, Mr Buxton, clearly had some reservations, since in the confidential report he wrote when Mr Ellis began to apply for headships, he had this to say: 'Mr Ellis is a likeable enthusiastic teacher always willing to experiment. He maintains constant interest among his pupils in a somewhat chaotic environment' ('somewhat chaotic' was later changed to 'fluid' at – since candidates see their confidential reports – Mr Ellis's request). It looks as though Mr Buxton, and perhaps even Mr Ellis himself, had a less sanguine view of what was going on at Charles Lamb than Mr Ellis's course director, Mr Watts.

Mr Ellis began his general statement in this way:

My whole teaching experience has been concerned with London children and has led me to the belief that the primary school in an urban situation should interest itself in the wider aspects of the life of its pupils, beyond the narrower meanings of the term 'educational'. A school should be aware of itself as part of a larger community and try to forge links with it, while remaining aware of both the limitations of such activities and a school's function of ensuring that important basic subjects are taught with efficiency.

All this is vague, not to say woolly, but it is clear that Mr Ellis was much taken with the notion of a community school. Among those whom Mr Watts brought into his course to give a number of lectures were a couple of headmasters who were running the sort of community school which, thought Mr Watts, Mr Ellis would probably have liked to run. One had become an inspector by the time of the inquiry; another, who lectured on community schools,

53

was Harry Stephens, headmaster of Gordon School in south London. Prior to that, Mr Stephens had run a school in Bethnal Green, where he had done some work with the Institute of Community Studies, set up by two popular sociologists, Michael Young and Peter Willmott.

In his lectures, Mr Stephens put a good deal of emphasis on 'goals'. Schools, he said, like any organisation, have one or more sets of 'goals', and they will be happier and more efficient places if the headteacher, staff and parents all have a say in the formulating of them. His approach owed a lot to basic organisation sociology and social psychology; his references were to the studies that were carried out in American industry (or, in one celebrated case, an American girls' school) between the wars. There, the underlying 'goal' of the experiments was greater productivity; in Mr Stephens' case, it was to avoid conflict. To that end, the co-operation of everybody concerned, over the formulation of goals and in other ways, was essential.

The importance of parental participation came home to Mr Stephens, he told us, when as a parent he realised that he was not getting from his child's headmaster the information to which he thought he was entitled. So, at Bethnal Green, he launched a big drive: opening up the school, sending out information sheets, questionnaires, and so on, trying to find out what the parents wanted and get them interested. At Gordon School, it was the same. Parents were in the school all day, they had a parents' room that was fully used (mainly as an exchange and mart) and Mr Stephens said that while the staff did not do any home-visiting, parents did; they were the antennae of the school. Certainly there was an ample two-way flow of information, but there was less evidence – on a brief visit – that participation extended to consultation, let alone decision making (or goal formulating). Some parents evidently had difficulty in getting their strongly held views on discipline through to Mr Stephens, and though a parent/teachers association had been formed, Mr Stephens had said he distrusted PTAs and was himself chairman of the one at Gordon School. Mr Stephens, in other words, was simply doing what teachers, as we have seen, have always done – manipulating parents in order to be able to run his school in his own way and according to his own lights.

Anybody in charge of an organisation often has to be somewhat devious in order to get his own way, and there was nothing remotely reprehensible in anything Mr Stephens said or did. But just as 'progressive' is a 'good' word, so 'manipulation' is almost by definition a 'bad' one: today everything must be done in the open, people must be told exactly what they are being asked to do and why. It is a little surprising, therefore, that Mr Stephens should have been asked to put across the idea and practice of a community school in a course such as Mr Watt's, where the whole emphasis was on open participation and non-directive methods. That Mr Ellis accepted the rhetoric of the course, so to speak, was clear from his application form; but that he did not take on board any of the practical lessons about implementing it was no less evident from his behaviour at William Tyndale, where not only were the aims of the school never clearly stated but bluntness to parents was erected into a virtue at the expense of winning their support. A clear statement of aims and a concern for parental involvement may not be sufficient to produce a community school (whatever that is), but their absence, as Mr Stephens pointed out, may well pave the way for open conflict.

Mr Haddow

Mr Haddow obtained his teaching certificate (with a distinction in teaching practice) in 1970 at Furzedown College in south London. There his tutor was George Mabbutt, who appears to have possessed many of the qualities of those who were responsible for the transformation of primary school teaching in this country: progressive in method, traditionalist in outlook and manipulative, where necessary, in practice. Mr Mabbutt had come to Furzedown after seven years as headmaster of Hotham Primary School in Putney on the understanding that he was to set up an integrated course, perhaps on the principle that if there were to be 'integrated days' in the primary schools, then the teachers had better be taught along 'integrated' lines as well. It was also a time when there was a good deal of student unrest at the college – though there is no suggestion that Mr Haddow was actively involved. The result was that Mr Haddow, whom Mr Mabbutt regarded as one of his two or three brightest students, had plenty of opportunity for discussion and argument with other students on the course and with his tutor. What, then, might the man whom Mr Auld described as having had, of all the teaching staff, 'the most profound influence upon the organisation and teaching methods and attitudes that were adopted at the Junior School in 1974 and 1975' have learnt from his time at Furzedown?

Mr Mabbutt was convinced that an open plan lay out and team-teaching were more effective ways of employing teachers' skills than traditional classrooms. 'Vertical grouping' – as in the reading scheme that Mr Ellis introduced during his first term at William Tyndale – he saw as both an 'organisational ploy and of educational advantage'. Infant schools were often organised along those lines, and Mr Mabbutt had a high regard for infant teachers. He felt that all students should do some teaching practice in infant schools – 'if you can teach infants, you can teach anywhere, including university'. And following that train of thought, he added: 'The great success of our primary schools is the emphasis on the children being involved in their own learning – and they don't get that again until they get to university.' On the same sort of principle, he was most insistent that his students should take responsibility for what they were doing – both then as students and later as teachers.

On the basis of Mr Haddow's performance at William Tyndale, it is reasonable to assume that none of this fell on deaf ears. On some points, though, tutor and student would more likely have been at loggerheads. On general philosophy, for example, Mr Haddow was never content with the way the principle of equal opportunity was interpreted in education. For him, it was not enough for education simply to be available; it was there to be used as a tool for social engineering, a means of changing society, and so on. Mr Mabbutt, on the other hand, had always taken a much more traditional stance: education did not need to be justified as a means to an end; it could be justified on its own terms. For him, the liberal position of simply opening the floodgates was enough.

In other respects, too, Mr Haddow must have been selective in what he chose to learn from Mr Mabbutt. While he was headmaster of Hotham, a mixed middle- and working-class school in Putney, Mr Mabbutt transformed it from a highly traditional one to a model progressive one; it was on the strength of his success there, in fact, that he got his job at Furzedown. But, he said, 'any success that I had as a headteacher was due to opening the doors to parents'. He emphasised to us, as he emphasised to his students, that the sort of thing he had done at Hotham could only be done by consent. If that meant being a bit devious, taking two steps back in order to take three forward later, then so be it. In the last analysis, if there was trouble, it could only come as a result of failing in one or more of the following ways: the programme not selling properly to the parents (though even he had quite a few parents taking their children away); putting it into practice too quickly (and at Hotham Mr Mabbutt had looked at his task in a ten-year perspective); or not carrying his staff with him.

On that last point, Mr Mabbutt ran into difficulties which were perhaps not unlike those Mr Ellis and Mr Haddow encountered in the person of Mrs Walker. When he arrived at Hotham, he found a young deputy head with strong views on order and discipline – monitors on the stairs, and so on. Instead of brusquely turning the place upside down, he bided his time and gradually won over the deputy to his point of view until, he said, 'with him we had walls knocked down, a library set up, a resources unit', and so on. He had some sympathy, though, for Mr Ellis. With the authority of the headteacher being increasingly questioned, it was no longer available as a weapon against the authoritarian styles of education from which it was derived; the headteacher was now in a glass bowl, and with everybody participating all the time, it was much more difficult to innovate, as he had done, by manipulating the system.

But Mr Mabbutt was successful in more directions that one. His deputy at Hotham, Ted Norfield, eventually became headmaster of John Milton School in a seedy part of Battersea. There, until he died in early middle age in 1970, he initiated and inspired a series of innovations that were, if anything, more radical than those Mr Mabbutt had introduced at Hotham. John Milton became something of an educational show-piece; Mr Pape, a senior ILEA inspector who gave evidence at the inquiry, quoted extensively from what was happening at that school in an occasional paper on 'co-operative teaching in the junior department' which was published by the ILEA in 1971. Before joining the staff of William Tyndale, Mr Haddow visited the school. Rather more of a coincidence, perhaps, is the fact that Mr Austin had taught there for four years. Now we shall take a brief look at John Milton, mainly through Mr Austin's eyes.

Mr Austin

When Mr Austin joined the staff in September 1974, he already had seven years' teaching experience. He had started teaching in Southampton, but then moved to London and John Milton School. After four years there he did a year's diploma course at the Froebel Institute before coming to William Tyndale. Thrust straight into the conflict with the managers at the beginning of that term, professional and political sympathies inclined him to side with Mr Ellis, Mr Haddow and the others, though he has since told us that he 'didn't realise to what extent the staff entertained no hope of avoiding open confrontation and how low

57

their morale was as a result'. He resigned as a full-time member of staff over their determination to resist an inspection of the school at all costs, even if it meant going on strike, but felt he could not abandon them altogether and came back part-time in September 1975. However, when the crunch came he left teaching altogether to take up a different career as a cartoonist. He gave brief evidence to the inquiry: Mr Auld found him a good witness; so did we.

Mr Pape described the team-teaching at John Milton as follows:

> On the top floor there are no separate classes; the teachers co-operate as a team. The floor is divided into areas according to use. There is an area for art, craft and general 'dirty' work. Another area serves for writing and quiet activities. There is a mathematics area in which all maths and science equipment can be found. A room containing movie projector, television and tape facilities is not in general use. The central area is a gathering place and contains the library.
>
> One teacher bases himself in each area and his work is determined somewhat by the area he is currently occupying. The teacher in the central area has the special responsibility of collecting those children who have finished their current work and need further stimulus.

That last job, which at William Tyndale was taken by Mr Haddow, was described in rather more graphic terms by Mr Austin as that of 'midfield sweeper'. He was there to look after the children who would not co-operative and who could, more easily perhaps than in a traditional classroom, make life impossible for everybody else and render the system unworkable. They had the same problems at John Milton as at William Tyndale, including their Homer Eliot and their 'broken furniture room'. But John Milton was a success, a show-piece to which visitors from all over the world were constantly being taken. What was the difference?

First, undistracted by external pressures, they all worked hard; the crucial 'midfield sweeper', for example, was able to stay at his post all the time. Secondly, they got the school's auxiliary helpers – secretary, dinner ladies, and so on – on their side by sharing the staffroom, the tea and coffee with them, and inviting them to staff meetings. These were also parents, so from the start some of those whose children the staff were most interested in helping knew what was going on, and had a chance to find out why the teachers were doing it. Moreover, through their strong links in the neighbourhood, these parents were able to give advance warning of any trouble that might be brewing – the exact opposite, in fact, of the picture that emerged at William Tyndale. It was not much, perhaps, but it was a good basis on which to build strong parent/school links.

Thirdly, John Milton had at the beginning a headteacher who had a very clear idea of what he was doing and why, and was able to express it. Mr Norfield used to say, for example, that, apart from giving the children an opportunity to find a teacher they were happy with, there were two reasons why he preferred team-teaching to more traditional classroom methods. It helped to minimise the bad effects of the high rates of teacher turnover in London schools, where it was not uncommon for a single class to have not just two or three but many teachers in the course of a year. Team-teaching could help ensure that there were always one or two teachers to provide some sort of continuity for the children. It also provided a cushion for the new, inexperienced and weak teachers, particularly those who might have difficulty in dealing with the more outrageous children.

It was also – and this was Mr Norfield's other reason for preferring team-teaching – a positive help in dealing with the most difficult children. In a traditional classroom, if a child runs out of it, there is nothing the teacher can do without abandoning the rest of the class. Where there is a team of teachers, and particularly a midfield sweeper in a bigger area, supervision becomes very much easier.

A more sophisticated version of that argument, with which Mr Austin at least was certainly familiar, would run like this. It is, in a sense, the obverse of the 'free choice' and 'total children's rights' approach which was so aggressively criticised at William Tyndale by Mrs Walker. If you allow children to roam where they want and do what they like, then there is no 'wrong-doing' left for them to do. There is no place a child can run to and say: 'This is my place, I know I shouldn't be here, but the teacher can't find me and I'm all on my own.' If he can go and play ping-pong virtually at will, then there is not the same temptation to say: 'Let's go and play ping-pong, I know we're not supposed to, but let's anyway.' In sociologists' jargon, this is known as 'legitimising' the space they escape to and the non-work things they do – which was the point at which parents, who could not possibly adopt a similar strategy in a small council home – often started to object. Obviously, too, there were limits: the boundaries of the school, for example, and disruptive behaviour. Not all children would respect those, but the theory was that in the end more would do so than respected the old classroom constraints.

Behind all this, though, there were two more fundamental differences between John Milton and William Tyndale. One concerned, so to speak, the name of the game. This was not children's rights, but social control; and this appeared to have been more openly admitted and discussed at the Battersea school than the Islington one. The prime object was to get as many children as possible obeying enough rules for the system to work. If that meant reducing to a minimum the number of rules (and at the same time the strain and drain on a teacher's energy) and manipulating the children by pretending to give them more freedom, it was of no consequence as long as the purpose of it was not lost sight of.

The other difference was one of time. At both schools, when all forms of manipulation had been tried and failed, the staff were liable to resort to conventional teachers' responses – shouting and losing their tempers. At John Milton that appeared to have happened no less than at William Tyndale in the early stages, but less and less as time wore on and everybody, children and staff, got used to the new approach. Mr Norfield had warned his staff that the first year would be 'hell'; Mr Ellis and his colleagues were never given a chance to get their first year going properly, let alone reap the benefits of it in subsequent years. Whether it would have made any difference if they had is, of course, another matter.

5. Representing the Community

As far as parents and managers were concerned, the story began in the playground. Early in the summer term of 1974 rumbles of discontent among the parents who gathered to collect or deliver their children reached the ears of two parents, Mrs Dewhurst and Mrs Gittings, who were also managers. Eventually, on 23 May – by coincidence the day after Mrs Walker had pinned her 'commentary' to the staff noticeboard – they reported the rumblings to the chairman of managers, Mrs Burnett, who, as a result of a visit she had recently made to the school to show another manager round, had herself become seriously concerned. Mrs Dewhurst was the elected representative of the junior school parents on the managing body (twelve parents had taken part in the vote) and she took her role sufficiently seriously both to attend a short ILEA course for managers and governors (which was mainly about the finances of schools) and to run a parents' newsletter about the school. She was therefore in constant touch with parents and staff and indeed had reported the parents' anxieties to Mr Ellis on several occasions, only to see them ignored.

Other schools, as we saw at the beginning of the last chapter, might have their share of disgruntled parents and they were certainly likely to have parents who were in a position to pick and choose their children's schools. Why did it all blow up at William Tyndale – particularly as the haemorrhage there did not really start until the end of that summer term? There was Mrs Walker, of course, and it is probably the case that most managing bodies, confronted by someone like her in the classroom, would have supported the headteacher in slapping her down. Indeed, many managing bodies would have been just as likely, on principle, to range themselves behind the headteacher and his staff as on the side of the parents. What was unusual at William Tyndale, perhaps, was the strength of the links between the managers and the playground, and when all the criticisms have been made about the recruitment, performance and behaviour of the managers, that should be remembered.

From the moment that Mrs Dewhurst and Mrs Gittings, quite properly, approached Mrs Burnett, the managers found themselves willy-nilly involved in a running battle with Mr Ellis and a large proportion of his staff. Mr Ellis, as headteacher, and Mr Haddow, as the elected teacher representative, were both members of the managing body (as were the headteacher and another teacher from the infant school), but a large part of the skirmishing took place outside the official managers' meetings, normally held once a term. Naturally, the more active managers tended to visit the school, but the meetings and discussions that took place with the staff at the school were only a small part of the story.

More important, the managers did not always appear to be sure which part they were playing. When Mrs Dewhurst and Mrs Gittings first approached Mrs Burnett, they may well have thought of themselves more as parents than as managers. Once a meeting between the three managers and Mr Ellis had been decided on and arranged for 7 June 1974, Mrs Gittings twice visited the school and the classrooms, much to the annoyance of Mr Ellis; on those occasions, presumably, she was acting as a manager.

Following the parents'/teachers' meeting of 9 July, from which Mr Haddow and several staff walked out, a special managers' meeting was held on 15 July at which Mr Rice, the district inspector, put forward his plans to solve the school's difficulties by giving it more money and resources. Unconvinced, Mrs Dewhurst and Mrs Gittings, joined now by another manager, Mrs Fairweather, decided to go and see Mr Rice on their own; they asserted at the inquiry that they were acting as managers and not parents – but might there not at the time have been just a tiny bit of confusion between their managerial and their parental hats? Later and more seriously, the confusion appeared to be between managerial and political hats.

With hindsight, it appeared both surprising and significant that at that special meeting those managers who felt strongly about what was happening in the school felt unable to speak their minds to Mr Rice in front of Mr Ellis and Mr Haddow. Such avoidance by the managers of direct confrontation seems to have been characteristic of their behaviour throughout most of the story. Indeed, such reserve had long tended to be a characteristic of managing bodies in general, many of whom still retained an excessive respect for headteachers. But it did not always have to be so; Councillor Albert Smith, one of the longest-serving Labour members of Islington borough council, talking about William Tyndale, told us the story of the time he was a manager for a brief period before the war. One day, he visited the school unannounced and, without warning anybody, told the caretaker to ring the fire-bell; he wanted to see how good the fire drill really was. He got into a lot of trouble from the headteacher and County Hall but, in telling the story, he dismissed all that with some contempt; as he said, when talking of the petition that was put round by a small group of managers in the spring of 1975 asking the authority to take some action over William Tyndale: 'Of course, I signed it . . . can't have that sort of thing [teachers preventing managers from visiting the school] . . . they are employees . . . managers are there to run the school with the divisional office . . . bloody cheek.'

In the days Mr Smith was talking of, managers were given no real power and precious little to do – apart from checking fire precautions, receiving accident reports and being responsible for the school premises. Nearly forty years later, any managing body faced with the sort of crisis that was threatening William Tyndale would have been in some difficulty. The ILEA, responding to pressure from Labour members on their return to power in 1970, had spelled out in some detail the responsibilities of managers, but it gave them no power to, and very little guidance on how to, exercise those responsibilities. As a consequence, the behaviour of the managers was partly due to ignorance of what they were able and expected to do, and partly due to the way they were appointed and the sort of people they were.

The 1944 Education Act required local education authorities to set up managing and governing bodies for their primary and secondary schools; it did not specify whom these bodies should be composed of nor did it define precisely what they should do or how they should do it. In the case of secondary school governors, the model articles of government did say that they must have the 'general direction of the conduct and curriculum of the school', but in the case of managers of primary schools everything was left to local discretion. However, from the time of the Plowden Report onwards, there had been increasing pressure to give a more clearly defined role to managing bodies. In 1973 the ILEA published its *Guide for Primary School Managers* incorporating the changed rules of management. Rule 2(a) ran as follows: 'The Authority shall determine the general educational character of the school and its place in the Authority's educational system. Subject thereto, the managers shall, in consultation with the headteacher, exercise the oversight of the conduct and curriculum of the school.'

In his report, Mr Auld made a great deal of those two sentences. In effect, he said, the authority had sought to delegate responsibility for what went on in the schools to the managers, but

63

without giving them the means to bear that responsibility effectively. In practice, he said, the ultimate responsibility still lay with the authority, since what it had delegated it could always revoke.

But since the authority was clearly unwilling to recognise that responsibility, there remained the very real difficulty, for the William Tyndale managers, of what they were to do if their 'oversight' led them to believe that all was not well. They could, of course, have passed a resolution which would have drawn the authority's attention to their concern, and it is perhaps surprising that no such formal resolution was passed until fully a year had gone by. The reason may well have been that it would have meant passing it at a meeting attended by the two members of staff most open to criticism, Mr Ellis and Mr Haddow. And after all, Rule 2 did say that managers should exercise their oversight 'in consultation with the headteacher'.

In practice, however, the authority was quickly made well aware of the managers' concern and did not need a managers' resolution to tell it that something was badly wrong. If the authority persisted in doing nothing – or not enough – what recourse did the managers then have? In his legal language, Mr Auld put the matter thus:

> The managers have only two courses of action properly open to them if they feel strongly about the matter. They are:
> (a) to make a complaint against the head teacher and/or members of his staff for inefficiency, misconduct or indiscipline under the authority's disciplinary procedures;
> (b) to invite the intervention of the Secretary of State, by requesting him to direct a local inquiry under Section 93 of the 1944 Act and/or to refer the matter to the Secretary of State under Section 67 of the 1944 Act for determination by him.

After it was all over, some members of the authority were to point out, almost plaintively, that none of the parties to the dispute had ever made a formal complaint to them. But the same considerations may have restrained, say, Mr Ellis from making a complaint about Mrs Walker as restrained the managers from making a complaint about Mr Ellis – namely, that it would have involved a head-on collision with someone they were supposed to be working with and would, into the bargain, have stirred up all sorts of mare's nests that they probably considered were best left undisturbed. As to the second option, both managers and teachers, independently of one another and for different reasons, proposed it in July 1975 as an alternative to an ILEA inspection and inquiry.

One reason, then, why several of the managers took to operating behind the scenes was that they were unwilling or unable to act 'corporately' – as Mr Auld sternly told them they should have done. But at least as important a factor was the way the managers were recruited to office. In the wake of the discretion left them by the 1944 Act, the one thing all local authorities seem to have agreed on is that appointments to managing bodies should be in the gift of the political parties represented on the authority's education committee. There was no logical or legal reason why that should have been so; there was nothing in the Act to stop local authorities asking a junior clerk to pick names out of the telephone directory. The upshot was that managers tended to be appointed from among those who were at least politically active enough to have joined their local constituency party, and the sort of people these were depended very much on the nature of the area – town or country, Labour or Conservative. In postwar Islington, dominated by the sort of Labour party we described in Chapter 2, retired trade union activists, when they could be prevailed upon to volunteer, figured prominently on managing bodies. In latterday Islington, with the Labour party heavily influenced by people such as the Fairweathers, the Mabeys and the Hoodlesses, it was the turn of the young middle-class professionals.

A number of events helped the transition to a more lively, interested type of manager. Schools such as Canonbury and William Tyndale, which for long had had to share a single managing body, gained the privilege of one all to themselves. This meant more managers had to be found – but it increased the chances of personal commitment and so made the job more attractive. The arrival of the comprehensive school meant that becoming a governor of a secondary school was a minor, but important, political act, and this must have had a spin-off effect on primary schools, even though managers of those schools still had a lot less responsibility than governors of secondary schools. Several of those who played an important part in the story of William Tyndale were also governors of secondary schools – Mrs Page and Mrs Burnett at Islington Green, for example, or Mrs Hoodless at Barnsbury Girls. In the aftermath of the Plowden Report, there was an added impetus to recruit people with qualifications other than purely political, such as social workers or probation officers (like Norma Morris, one of the Conservative nominees on William Tyndale) – or even parents.

All this made it slightly less hard to fill managerial vacancies, but never easy. In the case of Islington Labour Party, it was normally the job of the local (ward) party secretary, acting on behalf of the Labour party management committee. Any vacancy, whether officially an ILEA or a borough one (political nominees were more or less evenly divided between the two), was notified to him; as soon as he had found somebody, except in the rare cases of there being a surplus of volunteers, when it had to go up to the committee, the appointment was automatic. Early in 1975, however, at the height of the William Tyndale conflict, an attempt was made to transfer the power to appoint managers from the local management committee to the Labour group on the council; it was as though the Parliamentary Labour Party had decided to wrest a traditional prerogative from the National Executive Committee. The Labour group's victory was short-lived and had no important consequences for William Tyndale.

In this sort of atmosphere, though, it was hardly surprising that some of the more politically active managers were tempted to go to work behind the scenes. The first serious move of that sort – the visit by a group of managers to Mr Rice in July 1974 – was distinctly counterproductive in that, as soon as the teachers learnt of it, all trust between the two sides evaporated. However, it was not until the arrival on the managing body of Mrs Hoodless in January 1975 that such moves took an openly political turn. (Whether or not the appointment of Mrs Hoodless herself was one such move is a notion that even Mr Auld toyed with in his report, though he was unable to reach a conclusion on it.)

Mrs Fairweather, together with Mrs Gittings and Mrs Dewhurst (who was no longer a manager), had decided that the only way to get anything done was to do it themselves. She tried several times to get them an appointment with Mr Hinds at County Hall, but finally arranged it for the end of February through Mrs Hoodless's husband, Donald, who was a member of the GLC and so had easy access to Mr Hinds. Christina Miles, the infant school parent manager, was to have gone along with the other four, but backed down when told by Mrs Hoodless that the cover for the meeting was that they were to go as Labour representatives and that they would, therefore, have to be careful not to give the impression by their dress and appearance that they were simply a group of 'middle-class trendies' – a nice comment on themselves, their allies and their enemies. The approach was successful in that it prompted Mr Hinds to call for a report from the district inspector. When he had the report in his hands, Mr Hinds arranged a second meeting with the group of managers at the end of March, though this time Mrs Dewhurst's place was taken by Mrs Page, on Mr Hinds's invitation. It was at that meeting that the idea of a petition cropped up; immediately afterwards it was decided to do something about it.

Mrs Hoodless was due to attend a meeting of St Mary's ward Labour Party that evening, and she proposed, and got passed, a motion which noted the lack of confidence in the school as a result of the falling rolls and called on the ILEA to investigate its reorganisation as a single mixed infant and junior school. After that meeting, and armed with the resolution, she, and another ward councillor who had no direct connection with the school, Alan Pedrick, determined to organise a petition; they roped in to help them, besides the four active women managers, a councillor from another ward and three friends of Mrs Gittings. At the annual meeting of Islington Council, another manager, Mr Mabey, heard of the petition and decided to use it, together with some information on falling rolls provided by the authority, as the basis for a motion at the next regular managers' meeting. By bringing it into the open at a managers' meeting, Mr Mabey did something to bring all these unofficial activities back on the official rails, though his main purpose was to bring additional pressure on the teachers and the ILEA.

To some extent, all these managers were simply playing what they took to be the political game. By virtue of the fact that most of them were political nominees, they had some links with the local political network, whether at Islington or County Hall. David Howell of the London Institute of Education, co-author of a research study on school management and government prepared for the 1968 Report of the Royal Commission on Local Government, justified their behaviour in evidence to the inquiry by saying that since teachers could call upon their union, managers had to find their own allies, and it was natural that they should use their party links. That did not mean, he went on, that they should be beholden to those who appointed them, but he talked in terms of a special relationship between managers and the politicians who had put them there. This analysis appears to assume that relations between teachers and managers must necessarily be based on conflict – a view which does not clearly emerge from his published work. It may be that Mr Howell was unconsciously influenced by the fact that he was the father of a child at the infant school and husband of one of the organisers of the petition.

On the face of it, it is certainly reasonable to assume that, if managers are appointed through political channels, then they will, under pressure, behave like political animals. But would that assumption have appeared so plausible in the case, say, of a

William Tyndale managing body of the 1950s instead of the 1970s? Mrs Hoodless and her friends were not merely political animals; they were also social animals, of a particular kind. They used their political connections; but they also used their social ones. Most of those who figured prominently in the story knew one another – and many of the William Tyndale parents – socially. And if they did not know somebody they needed to know, they knew somebody else who did. Though they may not all have been on dinner-party terms with one another – there were fine gradations in those matters – they were certainly on children's tea-party terms. Both their political and their social lives were made manageable, and indeed possible, by the telephone.

This was one of the great strengths of those who formed the bristles of the new broom that had been sweeping Islington Labour Party for nearly a decade, and it took the old guard by surprise. Local Labour party politics have never incarnated an untarnished image of the popular will at work such as the term 'representative democracy' used to conjure up, but as a general rule pressures were applied and decisions taken in committees of one sort or another which, while hermetically sealed to outsiders, were open enough to members. The cabal-like telephone politics of the new activists – the 'highly educated' ones as they were called – were something new. Decisions were not merely taken prior to council meetings, but prior to group meetings as well. As Councillor Smith said to us, a trifle – but only a trifle – disingenuously: 'This is a new form of democracy; it is not the way we used to do it.'

Whether Councillor Smith and his ilk would have handled Mr Ellis and his colleagues any better, however, is a nice point. At least Mrs Hoodless and her fellow managers could say, as indeed they did when the inquiry was over and they had resigned, that if they had not acted in the way they did, nothing would have been done about the school at all. But need it all have happened? There was another major area of responsibility which fell to primary school managers, apart from all questions of 'oversight of the conduct and curriculum of the school', and that is the appointment of staff, and particularly the headteacher. How did Mr Ellis, Mr Haddow and Mrs McColgan, the three major *bêtes noires* of the managers, get their jobs in the first place? We shall take a look at that in the next chapter.

6. Appointing and Politicking

The ILEA procedure for the appointment of teachers and head-teachers was laid down in Rules 7 and 8 of the Rules of Management. In the case of an ordinary teaching post, the managers were responsible for selecting a shortlist for interview from among the applicants, though in practice this was often done by the head-teacher on his own. In the same way, the headteacher often made the final selection on his own, with or without the help of the chairman of managers. The headteacher's choice, though, had to be approved by the chairman whose 'action' in doing so had in turn to be ratified by the full managing body. That was the way internal promotions, responsibility posts, and so on were generally arranged, though the final decision could be, and quite often was, taken by the managing body.

In the case of headteachers, the ILEA had built in a few more safeguards. If the job was advertised as a 'service' one, only teachers who were on a special 'panel' could apply, though anybody could apply for one that was advertised as 'open'. Mr Ellis, for example, was put on the panel at his first attempt, following two interviews, the first with a group of district inspectors, the second with more senior inspectors and officers. From then on, the procedure was the same, whether it was an 'open' or a 'service' post. The chairman of the managers and ILEA officers together drew up a 'long' shortlist for interview by the managers; these then selected three to form a final shortlist which went to the authority's senior staff appointments subcommittee (some half-dozen members of the education committee) for a decision; the managers could, if they wished, 'star' one of the three names they put forward to indicate their preference.

The system was exceedingly amateurish. However much educational advice they may have had available to them, neither managers nor members of the ILEA subcommittee had any reason to be the least bit competent at probing candidates in the course of one short interview. They might have known something, for example, of what was involved in running a school, or introducing change into it; about different teaching methods and ways of organising and grouping children; about the political infighting within the National Union of Teachers and its local associations. But it was not a condition of their membership of their respective bodies. It was as though the senior management and chief executive of a firm were appointed by a group of part-time non-executive directors who did not necessarily have any expertise in the field in which the firm was operating. Moreover, in industry, mistakes could be remedied either by dismissal or by a golden handshake; no way had yet been found of getting rid of a bad headteacher except by 'promoting' him out of his job, possibly into one where he would be advising other headteachers.

The justification for involving managers so closely in the process was that they would, in theory, be the people likely to know the school best. However true that may have been in general – and a formal meeting once a term, even if regularly attended, was not the best basis for getting to know a school – it certainly was not true at the time of William Tyndale. Managers were appointed on a four-year renewable basis, and the summer of 1973 was a time when appointments came up for renewal. The Conservatives had been in power both on the ILEA and in Islington when the last batch of appointments had been made, and so there were a number of new faces in the autumn. In addition, the chairman, Mrs Donnison, resigned, so that the managers who appointed Mr Ellis in the autumn of 1973 and Mrs McColgan in the spring of 1974 were on the whole a different bunch from those who had appointed Mr Haddow and interviewed Mr Ellis first time round in the spring and summer of 1973.

The most influential person was, as always, the chairman. Mrs Donnison had been in charge when Mr Head had been appointed back in 1968 and had worked well with him ever since. As the wife of David Donnison, then director of the Centre for Environmental Studies and a former member of the Plowden Committee and chairman of the Public Schools Commission, Mrs Donnison had much to contribute. She had not wanted Mrs Burnett as her successor; her preference had gone to Stephanie Bromley, a young Labour Party member who was as tough-minded as she was, but Mrs Bromley declined. Mrs Burnett was also reluctant, but allowed herself to be persuaded. A former grammar school teacher with experience as a manager of Prior Weston Primary School in The Barbican and governor of Islington Green Comprehensive, she was, by all accounts, a conscientious – perhaps even to a fault – sort of chairman. One of the few remaining Conservative managers, however, felt that from the very beginning Mrs Burnett made insufficient effort to get to know and include in discussions the non-Labour managers.

How was it, then, that Mr Haddow, Mr Ellis and Mrs McColgan – a combination of strong personality, weak head-teacher and, as some might think, barrackroom lawyer – all came to find themselves at William Tyndale?

The appointment of Mr Haddow went through on the nod. That is to say, Mr Head chose him, Mrs Donnison, acting as chairman on behalf of all the managers, approved his choice, and the managers at their next meeting ratified it. Mr Haddow had been an excellent student, and had the best of references from his previous headteacher. Mr Head once said of Mrs Walker, whom he had appointed on a part-time basis four years earlier, 'Islington is Islington: any teacher with a year's experience is *experienced*', and similar considerations may have influenced his choice of Mr Haddow. In any case, the decision was in effect left to him, perhaps on the quite reasonable grounds that it could take one good professional to recognise another. Certainly, on past experience, Mrs Donnison had no cause to mistrust Mr Head's judgement.

In the case of Mr Ellis, the whole managing board played a full, if somewhat inglorious, role. The first advertisement, in the summer, when the job was advertised as a 'service' one, produced only a handful of applicants. William Tyndale was a small school (with a consequentially small salary attached to the job) in an unattractive area. It was also true that the high cost of living, and particularly of housing, in London meant that a dispro-portionately large number of teachers in London were either young and inexperienced or older, settled, classroom teachers; many of those of an age to set up house and start a family moved elsewhere, creating a general shortage of experienced staff as well as of headship material. In September, however, the job was advertised as an 'open' one, and nineteen candidates applied.

At each of the special managers' meetings called to interview candidates, only just over half of the full complement of managers turned up – fewer than usually attended routine meetings. Of the eleven present at the second meeting in November, only six had been managers the previous term and only five present at the first meeting in July. Three managers, by virtue of the parts they were to play in events later on, were conspicuous by their absence at one or both meetings: Mr Mabey, who did not attend either; Mrs Fairweather, who was present in November but not July; and Mr Tennant, a newly appointed manager who was to succeed Mrs Burnett as chairman fifteen months later, who failed to appear in November. It cannot be stressed too much that, at the time, appointing a new headteacher was far and away the single most important thing a manager was ever likely to be called upon to do.

Five candidates were called for interview in July, but one dropped out at the last minute, presumably because he had been offered a job somewhere else. Mr Ellis, who had already applied for the headship of half a dozen other schools, was one of the remaining four. Both meetings were attended by two representatives of the authority, including Mr Buxton, then district inspector. Mr Buxton's notes on Mr Ellis, taken at that first interview in July (and not, as Mr Auld wrote, at the November one) and used as the basis of his summing up to the managers, were put in as evidence to the inquiry. It is clear that to Mr Buxton, Mr Ellis appeared a pleasant, sensible, perceptive sort of fellow; 'sound' – a good, bureaucratic word – appears twice. But there was apparently nothing to mark him out as promotion material, no indication of what used to be known as 'officer-like qualities', and indeed one or two pointers in the other direction. Asked about his ability to 'control' (Mr Buxton's notes did not specify whether the reference was to staff or to children), Mr Ellis replied 'Yes – fool if I said otherwise'; asked about the reference in Mr Buxton's report on him to his 'lacking something in tact' he replied that bluntness could be the best form of communication.

In the light of Mr Ellis's later behaviour, it is worth comparing Mr Buxton's notes with the impression formed by Mrs Bromley, who was present at both interviews. Mrs Bromley described Mr Ellis as 'petulant . . . like someone summoned to the head's study, but not recognising the head's authority'. That description is not incompatible with some of the points Mr Buxton noted, but it is quite different from the overall tone of his notes. Together with Mr Buxton's willingness, referred to in Chapter 4, to change part of his confidential report at Mr Ellis's request, it raises the question of whether Mr Buxton may not, perhaps, have been the unintentional victim of what the sociologists call 'role conflict'. It was clearly part of Mr Buxton's job to help the managers pick out the three best candidates for the job. But what if that conflicted with another facet of his job, and one which was given particular emphasis at County Hall (as we shall see in Chapter 8) – that of being the teachers' friend, confidant and adviser?

However that may have been, the managers thought so little of the four candidates the first time round that they asked for a confidential report on only one of them, and that was not Mr Ellis. None of the managers we spoke to had a very clear recollection of that first meeting: Mr Ellis failed to impress. And that is interesting in itself. For example, one of the managers upon whom Mr Ellis apparently made no impression was Caryl Harter; the mother of two children at the school, she and her husband David, the director of the Islington Community Law Centre, were to be among Mr Ellis's most vocal supporters and advisers. There was clearly something wrong with a selection system that could not pick out someone whom a Mrs Harter would regard as potentially good any more than it could someone whom, say, Mrs Donnison might have regarded as potentially disastrous.

The second time round, in November, seven people were selected for interview, including Mr Ellis and Mrs Chowles, the deputy head of William Tyndale, who had not applied in the summer and was not seriously running this time. One or two of the managers who had seen Mr Ellis in July apparently thought he had 'improved' – though whether that meant in potential as a headteacher or in performance before a board of unskilled interviewers was not clear. Mrs Dewhurst and Mrs Gittings were favourably impressed. But the dominant consideration at that meeting was the need to come to some sort of decision; the school was without a head and Mrs Chowles was, on her own admission, not happy holding the fort. But the lack of enthusiasm of the managers can be gauged from the fact that besides Mr Ellis and another deputy head, they put forward as their third choice someone who was not even a practising teacher but the warden of a youth centre.

The managers were not agreed in preferring one of the three to the other two, so none of the names was 'starred' as being the managers' first choice. However, at least one manager was quite clear whom she did not want. Next day, Mrs Bromley telephoned Mrs Burnett, who as chairman would be representing the managers at the final meeting of the 'appointment of headteachers and principals section of the staff and general subcommittee of the education committee of the ILEA', and said 'Don't you dare let Ellis get it at County Hall'. According to Mrs Bromley, Mrs Burnett agreed, but explained later that the other two candidates performed so badly that there was in effect no option but to aquiesce in the appointment of Mr Ellis. Anyway, even after telephoning Mrs Burnett, Mrs Bromley was still not satisfied, since she voiced her fears to her sister, Mia Beaumont, who also lived in Islington but had Conservative connections. Mrs Beaumont in turn spoke to Jenny Baker, another neighbour who also happened to be a Conservative co-opted member of the ILEA. Mrs Baker was sufficiently concerned to exercise her right to sit in, as a non-voting member, alongside the five full members on the meeting of the appointments subcommittee at County Hall.

What worried Mrs Baker most, at that final interview, was Mr Ellis's apparently muddled thinking over the concept of a headteacher's responsibility. He talked very well, she told us; indeed, one of his answers at his first interview in July which had prompted Mr Buxton to describe him as 'sound' in his notes was his description of the role of the headteacher as 'the last line of responsibility'. But Mrs Baker gained the impression at County Hall that he tended to disappear into 'a dream world – a sort of teachers' commune where there would be no head and all teachers would take decisions together'. She pressed him on this, but she felt he evaded the issue. However, it was clear that the youth centre warden was seen as a 'hopeless' candidate and many of those present apparently took against the other deputy head, a middle-aged woman who gave the impression of being rather prissy. Mr Buxton's summing up pointed strongly in the same direction so, because of the pressure to make an appointment, Mr Ellis got the job.

The third appointment of importance for which the managers were responsible was that of Mrs McColgan in the spring of 1974, at the end of Mr Ellis's first term as headteacher. Mrs McColgan's arrival was important for two reasons. She was very keen on teacher participation and it was largely under her influence that staff meetings moved as quickly as they did towards what Mrs Baker had taken to be Mr Ellis's ideal of a teachers' commune. Mr Ellis, of course, in the course of his cross-examination at the inquiry, denied that matters ever reached that stage and implied that throughout he had remained firmly in control. The weight of evidence, however, pointed to Mr Ellis being manipulated by his staff rather than the other way about. The other reason was that Mrs McColgan was a fighter. Ever since she had been dismissed from her job at Highbury Quadrant in 1969 she had not only had difficulty in finding jobs but had been in almost continuous dispute with the authority over the terms and conditions of the jobs she did get. Wherever she saw her own or teachers' rights under attack, her instinct was to stand and fight, and there is little doubt that she stiffened the resolve of the William Tyndale teachers at times when some of them might have been ready for compromise. She was also responsible for one of the rare flashes of wit in an otherwise rather dreary story – a notice in the staff commonroom which read, 'You may be paranoiac, but that doesn't mean they're not after you'.

The appointment was made at a special meeting of the

managers called to interview Mrs McColgan and one other candidate (only nine managers attended). There was a country-wide shortage of qualified maths teachers, and by all accounts Mrs McColgan was far and away the better of the two candidates. Moreover, she had been teaching for thirty years and she turned out to be an excellent, conscientious, middle-of-the-road classroom teacher who was said by one of her colleagues at the school to have put in more extra hours, in holidays and so on, than any other member of staff. On strictly professional grounds, her appointment was amply justified. But were strictly professional considerations the only ones the managers should have taken into account? In an ambiguous sentence in his report, Mr Auld wrote that 'some managers ... had some knowledge of [Mrs. McColgan's] previous disputes with the Authority'. That would certainly have been true of the two teacher managers, Mr Ellis and Mr Haddow; the dispute was well known to Islington teachers, if only because the North London Teachers' Association had espoused her cause. Besides, according to Mr Buxton in his evidence to the inquiry, when Mr Ellis in his capacity as acting head of Charles Lamb was offered the chance of taking on Mrs McColgan, he rejected the offer out of hand: he wouldn't have her there at any price, he was reported as saying. Mr Haddow, it will be remembered, had met Mrs McColgan – and signed a motion of support for her – when she had visited the school to present her case towards the end of the previous year. Mr Buxton was not present at the interview and did not say anything about her disputes with the authority in his report on her, though he had known she was in for the job. With William Tyndale in a precarious position under a new headteacher who had barely had time to establish himself, was it in the best interests of the school to take on somebody with Mrs McColgan's track record? Did Mr Buxton who, though no longer district inspector, was the person best placed to consider the interests of both the school and Mrs McColgan, perhaps lean over backwards to be fair to Mrs McColgan, mindful of her accusations that the authority was persecuting her? Mrs McColgan herself told the managers that she had been in dispute with the authority, but they apparently did not think it worth pressing the point. If in the end, therefore, they did not fully appreciate the nature of the disputes Mrs McColgan had had, then they had only themselves to blame.

The method of appointment adopted by the ILEA was not the only possible one. Some other authorities had joint committees where managers or governors were outnumbered by officers of the authority, but, as we have seen, that would not be enough to guarantee that the school's interests should be put before all others. The fundamental problem was that there was no objective way by which a teacher's performance could be assessed: he writes nothing, cures nobody, does nothing but teach. All that an interviewing body, however constituted, ever had to go on was the previous headteacher's testimonial, the confidential report by an inspector, and the candidate's own application form and performance at the interview. In the three cases we have discussed, it could be argued that those were not enough. The weakness of the system, however, did not stem just from the inexpertness of the interviewers; the whole question of appointments goes right to the heart, as we have seen, of the inspectors' job. We discuss this more fully in Chapter 8.

7. A Divided Authority

Within a year of Mr Ellis taking over the headship of William Tyndale, the teachers were not fully in control of what was going on in the school, the managers were certainly not in control of what the teachers were doing, and the two sides were at logger-heads. On the fringes were the parents, whose dissatisfaction after only a term of Mr Ellis had sparked the conflict off; the local politicians who, by hyperactivity (in Islington) or by inactivity (at County Hall), made a bad situation worse; and the teachers' union whose right hand, as we shall see in Chapter 9, did not know what its left was doing – and if it had, would probably not have approved. In the middle, and most unwilling either to hold the ring or stop the fight, was the authority with its three faces: the politicians on the education committee whose effective leader, for the purposes of this story, was Mr Hinds; the divisional and administrative officers under the education officer, Dr Briault; and the inspectors, under the chief inspector, Dr Birchenough.

A year later a public inquiry was trying to determine the true nature and function of this three-headed hydra. It was the first time that the workings of a local education authority, and the relationship of the various parts to one another, had been subjected to close public scrutiny. A spotlight was turned on the confusion that surrounded the whole topic among the public, the professionals and even the representatives of the authority them-selves. Nobody really knew whom to go to for effective action. The managers, at the beginning of the troubles, turned first to the district inspector, Mr Rice, and then by more or less devious means to the top politician, Mr Hinds. The teachers, too, at different times, appealed to both Mr Rice and Mr Hinds, while Miss Hart, the headteacher of the infant school, voiced her complaints first to Mr Rice and then to the divisional represen-tative of the County Hall administration, Mr Wales. None of them quite knew what he or she expected Mr Hinds, Mr Wales or Mr Rice to do, and that was hardly surprising since the one thing the inquiry made perfectly plain was that the representatives of the authority were not agreed among themselves; not even the three inspectors who gave evidence were able to describe their job in the same way. Partly this was due to personality clashes and office politics; a far more important cause, though, was a fundamental uncertainty, inherent in the whole British education system, about what a local authority and its various parts were really in business to do.

The conventional view, not just in London but throughout the country, was aptly put by Mr Hinds at the inquiry. 'In the English system,' he declared, 'the attitude of the education authorities is one of leaving teachers to teach and managers to manage, relying on a mutual confidence which in experience is rarely shown not to exist.' That in its turn depended on an interpretation of the 1944 Education Act which limited the task of an education authority to providing an education service. More specifically, that was generally taken to mean providing the particular services – buildings, teachers, ancillary workers, administrative back-up – without which there could be no education service. On this view, the quality of the service was measured by the amount of resources put into it; thus, the authority which built the newest schools, employed most teachers for fewest pupils, and spent the greatest sums on books and materials, was reckoned to be providing the best education.

Like many others who have looked at education from the outside, Mr Auld was not impressed by the assumptions on which this view was based. In his report, to define an authority's function, he turned to the exact wording of the Act and concluded that local education authorities were in business to provide an 'efficient' education 'suitable to the requirements' of the children. Taken literally – and Mr Auld meant it to be taken literally – that meant that the authority could not just let teachers and managers get on with it together; it could not hide behind its rules of management to delegate responsibility for 'the conduct and curriculum of the school'; it had itself to be responsible for what went on in the classroom.

Between Mr Hinds's view and that of Mr Auld a great gulf was fixed. It was not simply a question of philosophy or outlook, though it was partly that. It also affected the job that the authority's officers had to do and the way in which they were expected to do it. On Mr Hinds's view, the central task of County Hall, like that of any large organisation, was a straightforward management one: the collection, organisation and distribution of resources. In that sense, the administrators and divisional officers, from the education officer down to the lowliest clerk, with their clearly defined hierarchy of responsibility, were like the line managers of industry. William Tyndale Junior School could do with another £700 being spent on it? Right, the assistant education officer (primary) was the person to see that the school got it. Those in the lower grades did not even need to have any educational expertise. Behind this core structure were a number of specialist back-up services, such as research and planning. One such was the inspectorate, whose job, on this view, was limited mainly to providing advice and in-service training to teachers. The Auld view, on the other hand, with its emphasis on 'efficiency', raised the spectre of that other industrial function, quality control – and that way, Hamlet might have said if he had been an education officer, madness lies: what do you test, how do you test it, who tests it and what sanctions do you keep in reserve? Some form or other of quality control had traditionally been one of the main functions of the inspectorate – as its name suggested; and we shall be looking more closely at that in the next chapter. The main point here is that whereas the Auld view demanded of the inspectorate that it assess, judge and, in the last analysis, act as the agents of control of what went on in the schools and classrooms, the Hinds view did not.

The Hinds view of the way the English education service functioned was largely shared by London's teachers, administrators and inspectors. County Hall, the biggest local educational bureaucracy in the country, may not have been too well liked by the teachers, and Mr Hinds may not have been too popular with some of his junior officers. There is no doubt that the non-appearance at the inquiry of both his chief officer, Dr Briault, and his leader, Sir Ashley Bramall, left Mr Hinds in rather an exposed position. But Mr Hinds, an ex-clergyman and trained youth worker, had a vast experience of London education – he had been a member of the schools subcommittee in 1965 when the authority closed down Risinghill Comprehensive and he had been its chairman since 1970. He was well placed to form a view of the workings of the service and his view coincided with the way in which the balance of power between the administrators and inspectors at County Hall had been shifting over the preceding twenty years.

The man most responsible, in effect, for downgrading the inspectorate and upgrading the administrators was Dr Briault, who first joined London's administration in 1948 as an inspector and became deputy education officer eight years later. He then waited fifteen years before stepping into the top job. When he came to London, the authority had a dual career structure that was virtually unique. In most authorities, the chain of command went down from the chief education officer through his deputy, possibly one or more senior assistant education officers (as in London), and assistant education officers down to the divisional officers. Any inspectors, organisers or advisers – outside London the titles were frequently interchangeable – may have had their own little hierarchies, but few had, like London, a career structure which paralleled that of the administrators virtually to the top. Two things made the London inspectorate particularly powerful in the early 1950s. One was that, though the chief inspector remained technically subordinate to the deputy education officer, his salary was put on a par with that of the deputy. The other was that middle and senior appointments in the administrative structure were generally made from among those on the inspectorate ladder. Thus most assistant education officers and above had started bureaucratic life as inspectors (before that, following the general pattern, they would have been teachers and frequently headteachers). Dr Briault himself came up that way, from teaching to the inspectorate to deputy education officer.

During his long spell in the deputy's chair, Dr Briault acquired a reputation for being a brilliant administrator – 'a good man with a room full of paper', as one local politician described him – and for a strong personal commitment, which he tended to insist should be shared by his subordinates, to particular education policies. Partly as a result, he accumulated a great deal of power. One of the criticisms that could be heard of him in County Hall at the time of the William Tyndale affair was that, having as deputy made sure that as many strings as possible ended up in his hand, he had taken them all across with him on his promotion. All major decisions had to go up to him. And, it was believed largely as a result of his influence, inspectors could no longer be quite so sure that senior administrators would be appointed from their ranks. An example was Patricia Burgess, a career administrator who was appointed assistant education officer (primary) in preference to George Andrews, one of the team of primary inspectors.

All this had some practical consequences for William Tyndale. When Mr Hinds was first alerted, in the summer of 1974, by Mrs Page to the fact that all might not be well at the school, he asked one of the senior line managers responsible, Miss Burgess, to look into it. She asked the district inspector, and that is how Mr Rice came to write his first report on William Tyndale. He sent it to Miss Burgess, with a copy to his chief inspector, Dr Birchenough, rather than, as would at one time have been thought more correct, the other way round. Dr Birchenough took no action on it anyway, any more than he did on the many letters of complaint from parents; these went to TS13, the disciplinary department at County Hall, which kept Dr Birchenough informed

80

but did not consider it necessary to point out that the number of complaints about William Tyndale was unusually large.

However that may be, Mr Rice's report, which was far from alarmist in tone, suggested putting more resources into the school, and Miss Burgess saw to it that those extra resources were made available. Mr Hinds, however, never saw the report, and Miss Burgess took little further action. But she did mention it to her immediate superior, William Braide, senior assistant education officer (schools), and a former inspector. Mr Braide, however, was on the point of retiring; his post was redefined and the responsibility for schools which he had held was brought within the ambit of Mr Newsam's brief as deputy education officer. Whether or not Mr Braide put Mr Newsam in the picture about William Tyndale – and we have been unable to establish for certain that he did – Mr Newsam was fully occupied at the time in negotiating the disappearance of many of London's best-known grammar schools. Though there were perfectly good reasons for this emphasis on secondary reorganisation (it was one of the policies to which Dr Briault was particularly committed), a number of people felt that primary schools had had to suffer as a result, and that this had a direct bearing on what happened at William Tyndale. Paradoxically, by an accident of politics, the responsibility for the relative neglect of London's primary schools could be laid at the door of the Plowden Committee. By reporting in 1967, they gave London's incoming Conservative administration all the incentive they needed to put the main thrust of their policies on primary education. If Labour had won the local elections, they would probably at least have spread their enthusiasm more evenly over primary and secondary education. As it was, when Labour got back in 1970, they concentrated almost exclusively on secondary reorganisation, to the detriment, in terms of both manpower and attention, of London's primary schools – though whether that in fact made much difference to William Tyndale is open to doubt.

The story of Mr Rice's first report shows what could happen when a policy shift occurred in a giant bureaucracy without anybody having any very clear idea of why or how. The influence of the inspectorate at County Hall was being diminished at the same time as the inspectorate was becoming keener to relinquish a good deal of its own power over teachers. Though historically related, the two processes were discrete. A number of petty rivalries and jealousies arose, inevitably fouling up some of the lines of communication. By the time William Tyndale came along, as Mr Auld said, 'the Authority was not equipped to make the right corporate judgement about the School and the action required to deal with it. There were too many individuals involved, and too many different levels and lines of responsibility, for them to be able to deal efficiently with the problem as a collective body.'

The situation was made worse by a good deal of unrest among the middle tiers of administrators at County Hall by the policy of participation and open decision making initiated by the Labour group when they came to power in 1970, partly in response to the Liberal revival. Parents, in particular, were consulted about a growing number of issues: how should transfer from primary to secondary schools be organised? should secondary schools be small neighbourhood ones or large comprehensives with big sixth forms, and so on? The bureaucrats found all this, and particularly the fact that they were expected to take account of the answers even when they went contrary to previous policy, hard to take. It is difficult, in fact, to resist the impression that the way the inspectorate and the politicians were left to carry the can at the inquiry unaided by anyone of any importance in the administration was no accident; a number of scores were being settled.

However, though Mr Hinds did a very good job at the inquiry of putting into words the pragmatic English approach to running education – of translating praxis into theory, in other words – he still left unanswered the question of what ought to happen when things went wrong. He bravely asserted at one stage that he was constantly in touch and could expect to be informed within two hours if anything drastic was happening, but in the case of William Tyndale that patently did not happen. Indeed, on nearly every occasion in which he was brought into the story, he left himself open to criticism – and indeed was severely criticised by Mr Auld in his report. Having asked Miss Burgess for a report on the school, he failed to insist on seeing it; three months later, in September 1974, he failed to respond positively to a letter from Mr Ellis asking him to intervene in an increasingly open and bitter dispute; having agreed to see, on an unofficial basis, a group of managers in February 1975, he promptly asked for another report from Mr Rice, but misinterpreted it when he met the managers again a month later and – much more seriously and quite erroneously – left them with the impression that he could only act if there was evidence of community concern, that is, a petition; and so on, right through to July when his attempt to call managers and teachers together came too late to do any good. He misled the teachers in telling them that Mr Rice's report showed there was nothing educationally wrong with the school and misinformed the managers over the scope of an ILEA inspection.

Clearly, then, neither the administrators nor the politicians were in a position to receive an early warning – or to recognise one when it came – or to take appropriate fire-fighting action when trouble broke out. That left the third head of the hydra, the inspectors, who are perhaps the least known and least understood part of the education service; even teachers frequently know very little about them. Yet they were the principal link between a school and the authority, and were also available to offer help and advice to managers. They deserve a chapter to themselves.

8. A Look at the Inspectors

Had the ILEA's politicians and administrators realised in time the gravity of what was happening at William Tyndale, there would still have remained the question of what to do about it. In theory, that was not their concern, but that of the third face of the ILEA – the inspectorate. The catch-all answer, in the words that cropped up several times, usually in the mouths of managers or those Islington politicians who knew a little about education, was: 'Send for Dr Birchenough and his troops.' But though their name certainly implied some sort of authority-boosting role, military metaphors of that nature were not at all to the liking of the inspectors themselves. After all, responsibility for the organisation and teaching in all schools lay with the headteacher (who, in most primary schools, did not even have any teaching duties). Should not therefore teaching be regarded in the same light as medicine, with teachers able to hide behind the pedagogical equivalent of clinical freedom? If not, what questions can be asked of a teacher, and who is to ask them?

The true nature of the inspectorate's role was hedged about with doubts and uncertainties, compounded by the inspectors' own ontological hesitations and concern for professional niceties. London's inspectorate was, in many respects, closely modelled on the national inspectorate at the Department of Education and Science. In order to understand the difficult position in which Dr Birchenough, who had come to the ILEA from the DES, found himself, we must take a look at Her Majesty's Inspectors (HMIs, as they are known). In the context of William Tyndale, they were like the dog that didn't bark. Indeed, throughout all the hullabaloo, from the day Mr Ellis took up his post until the day Mr Auld handed over his report two and a half years later, a face was missing, a chair was empty – that of the DES. Towards the end of the affair both managers and teachers, it is true, invoked the minister or his mandarins, but at that stage these were little more than pious hopes that a *deus ex machina* would come down from the clouds and sort things out in a way favourable to the petitioner.

The DES, however, had no need of a formal request to

intervene. The 1944 Education Act stated that 'any local education authority *may* cause an inspection to be made of *any* educational establishment maintained by the authority. . .'. Where the government is concerned, though, the wording leaves no room for ambiguity. 'It *shall* be the *duty* of the Minister to cause inspections to be made of *every* educational establishment at such intervals as appear to him to be appropriate, and to cause a special inspection of any such establishment to be made whenever he considers such an inspection to be desirable.' (our italics in both cases) Whatever caveats may be made about the intentions of the lawmaker – he was thinking mainly of secondary schools – or about the way custom and practice have modified the law, HMIs were organised so as to enable them to give effect to the Act. Every school in the country, including London schools, was the responsibility of one or other of the 500 or so HMIs; the one responsible for William Tyndale was John Woodend. But, though they were kept informed, the DES took no action over William Tyndale; they did not visit the school and, apart from a formal answer to a Parliamentary Question, they made no public statement and gave no evidence to the inquiry. It is true that none of the parties to the inquiry called the DES as a witness, but a decision not to intervene over William Tyndale in any way at any time must have been taken, so a retired senior inspector told us, at the highest level.

There were plenty of reasons for the DES to keep its collective head in the position it has always preferred – well below the parapet. At the time of the Plowden Report in 1967 only a third of all local authorities had a recognisable inspectorate of their own, and some of these were very small. London, however, which had been one of the first to set up its own in 1872, had some eighty inspectors, more than twice as many as the next one, Birmingham, and from four to ten times as many as most. When R. A. (now Lord) Butler, the moving spirit behind the 1944 Act, brought the Board of Education back from Bournemouth to London and transformed it into a ministry, he made it quite plain that his inspectors were going to inspect, and that meant London schools as well. However, practice soon reverted to what it had been before Mr Butler, and London was left alone. There was also the delicate question of Dr Birchenough, London's chief inspector who had come to the job in 1973 after thirteen years as an HMI, five of those as a chief HMI. It might have been thought at the DES that Dr Birchenough would have a difficult enough task establishing himself and persuading his new colleagues that he was not about to transform them all into HMIs without having his old colleagues breathing down his neck at the first signs of a spot of bother. Still, the DES was behaving as though the very existence of London's inspectorate enabled it to pass the buck to the ILEA just as the authority's rules of management provided Mr Hinds with the perfect means of passing the buck on to the headteacher and the managers.

Everybody involved found support and comfort in the report of the 1968 Parliamentary Select Committee on Her Majesty's Inspectorate which recommended, among other things, that in the passage of the 1944 Act quoted above the 'duty' of the Secretary of State to cause inspections to be made should be replaced by 'right'; that full-scale formal inspections should be discontinued; and that a greater share of inspection should be left to local authorities – though 'the Secretary of State should, however, retain his right to require a formal inspection of a school by HM Inspectorate, particularly if so requested by a local education authority or a teachers' organisation'. No changes in the law were made following that report, though most of those recommendations have, in practice, been adopted.

However, in theory at least, though HMIs welcomed the recommendations as much as anybody, they left the DES in a rather difficult position because, from its earliest beginnings in 1839 – six years after the first grant for education had been voted by Parliament – the inspectorate was directly linked to the disbursement of public money for schools. To put it crudely, the corps was created as an upper-middle-class elite, recruited until 1926 by patronage and until very recently almost exclusively from among the products of the public schools, with the task of supervising the education of the poor by lower-middle-class teachers. The means by which this control was to be exercised was the 'right of inspection'. This was then, and still is today, the only formal means by which an account by professionally qualified educationists can be rendered of the way the taxpayers' money that has been allocated for education is actually being spent in a particular school. The refusal of the William Tyndale teachers, by going on strike, to allow a proper full inspection to take place was not only a snub to their employers; it directly attacked the last bastion, already seriously weakened, of teacher accountability.

Right from the beginning, though, the primary control function was disputed. In a passage that has often been quoted with approval by inspectors and appeared on the first page of the report of the 1968 Parliamentary Select Committee on Her Majesty's Inspectorate, Sir James Kay-Shuttleworth in 1840 sent the following instructions to the handful of inspectors of the time:

It is of the utmost consequence that you should bear in mind that this inspection is not intended as a means of exercising control, but of affording assistance; that it is not to be regarded as operating for the restraint of local efforts, but for their encouragement; and that its chief objectives will not be attained without the co-operation of the school committees – the Inspector having no power to interfere, and not being instructed to offer any advice, or information excepting where it is invited.

Twenty years later, the nineteenth-century backlash appeared with the report of the Newcastle Commission which stated, in part:

There is only one way of securing this result [the efficient teaching of every child] which is to institute a searching examination by competent authority of every child in every school to which grants are to be paid, with the view of ascertaining whether these indispensable elements of knowledge are thoroughly acquired, and to make the prospects and position of the teacher dependent to a considerable extent on the results of this examination.

The last clause had a permanent effect on the attitudes of those involved in the English education system. Since teachers' salaries were paid out of the grants, it was tantamount to a system of payment by results. The National Union of Teachers, formed in 1870, fought its first bitter campaign on this issue and finally succeeded in getting it repealed thirty-six years later in 1898.

The report of the Newcastle Commission had spoken of 'efficient teaching'. This term, which was picked up by Mr Auld in his report, appeared in the 1944 Act, but it was also one of the things HMIs looked for from the beginning of the century when one of their main tasks became the inspection and, if satisfactory, recognition of secondary schools and further education colleges. It was still being used in circulars and administrative memoranda in the 1960s. But with the abolition of payment by results, any hope of establishing nationally agreed criteria of efficiency vanished. In *The Handbook of Suggestions for the Consideration of Teachers in Elementary Schools*, published in 1905, part of the preface read as follows: 'The only uniformity of practice that the Board of Education desires to see in the teaching of Public Elementary Schools is that each teacher should think for himself and work out for himself such methods of teaching as may use his powers to the best advantage and be best suited to the particular needs and conditions of the school.' Precisely, one might add, what Mr Ellis and Mr Haddow considered they were doing.

For the rest of this century, attempts to control what was taught in schools by central government were, with the occasional hiccough, progressively replaced by the constraints on teachers imposed by examinations (including the 11-plus), the interlocking structure of the system from infant school through to higher education, staffing – and even, as William Tyndale showed, what the public would bear. One result, though, was that no agreed criteria were established for the ill-defined terms of the 1944 Act, 'efficient education' and 'suitable to the requirements of the children'. Thus, subject only to the constraints we have mentioned, the English teacher in the English classroom has enjoyed a remarkable degree of freedom in what he teaches and how. Under the slogan of 'autonomy in the classroom' teachers and the NUT have been quick to defend these freedoms whenever they have appeared to be threatened. One example is revealing. In the early 1960s there was a move to set up a 'curriculum study group' within the DES. An alliance was formed of local education authorities and the NUT to scupper the proposal, but the final outcome was a teacher-controlled Schools Council in which not even the local authorities had an effective say. And the same slogan served to rally the William Tyndale staff and their local union association against what they saw as excessive classroom visiting by the school's managers. Over the years, however, teachers in general and particularly their unions have been more concerned to defend that autonomy than to use it.

Where teachers fear to tread, though, the inspectorate stepped in. Having been well and truly tarred with the payment by results brush – they had been the agents, though not the instigators, of that unfortunate policy – HMIs tended to put a greater distance between themselves and central government and to move closer to teachers in an advisory and supportive capacity. Much of the reform of primary school teaching methods since the war could be attributed to the work of HMIs. More recently, particularly under William Elliott, senior chief inspector from 1968 to 1972, HMIs had begun to view themselves once again as more at the service of the DES. They had become more policy-oriented, prepared to drop everything and prepare an instant report on whatever might be the DES nightmare of the moment – the raising of the school-leaving age, sixth-form reorganisation, attainment testing, and so on. That could lead them once again into areas where their concerns clashed with teachers' interests but, on the whole, the NUT at least appeared to like what HMIs had been doing. In 1894, just a few years before the abolition of payment by results, the NUT, in its evidence to the Bryce Commission, made it clear that it would like to see HMIs replaced by locally based inspectors. Three-quarters of a century later, at the time of the 1968 select committee, the NUT were singing the opposite tune: much to their surprise, HMIs found themselves being complimented at the expense of local authority inspectors.

One reason for this lay, as so often in education, in a confusion of roles. In a report to his committee in April 1976, just after the inquiry had finished, Dr Birchenough defined the dual aspects of his inspectors' jobs:

(a) to advise members and officers of the ILEA and to give them information on the state of education in the area for which the authority is responsible;
(b) to give a service to the staff of ILEA schools and colleges by advising them and helping them in their professional development.

Inspections, Dr Birchenough believed, could serve in both cases. But however much they might provide back-up services and in-service training and generally aim to be the teachers' adviser, helper and friend, they were also the only source for the reports that always accompanied a teacher's application for promotion or another job. There was a fundamental contradiction there, which in part accounted for the fact that, outside London, so few authorities had developed their inspectorate to anything like the same extent. It was not reasonable to expect a teacher in difficulties to turn for help to an ex-teacher – for nearly all inspectors, organisers and advisers were recruited from within the profession – whose impression could make or break his career. Mr Ellis, for example, complained at the inquiry that Mr Buxton's report on his teaching at Charles Lamb was based on a visit of only ten minutes. That sort of mistrust could be overcome if the inspector was able to visit the school regularly and get to know the staff well; if the initial call for help had to be made by letter or on the telephone, it was much more difficult. All this meant, among other things, that the inspectors themselves were all the more eager to emphasise what they called the 'supportive' parts of their job and to play down its 'judgemental' aspects.

A look at the reports which the inspectors wrote about William Tyndale will illustrate this. The first report, dated 8 July 1974, came from Mr Rice, the district inspector, following a request from Mr Hinds through the assistant education officer (primary). The report was short and contained no reference either to Mr Haddow's fourth-year class or to the concern which had been expressed by parents, managers and the headteacher and staff of the infant school. There was, it is true, a bald statement that there was to be a meeting of parents the following day and a special managers' meeting the following week. But though Mr Rice did not actually send the report until after that parents' meeting on 9 July, he did not amend it to take account of the meeting, and the planned walk-out by Mr Haddow and his followers, any more than he had mentioned the uproar at the 13 June meeting.

Mr Rice referred only fleetingly to the abortive reading scheme which Mr Ellis had sought to introduce in his first term: 'He has tried to introduce a form of co-operative teaching with children being sent to different teachers in small groups. . . . The staff are relatively inexperienced and it might have been wiser initially to make sure of the qualities of the staff before implementing new organisation.' There is a hint of criticism there, but all put carefully into the past tense, with nothing to indicate that Mr Ellis ought perhaps to have changed his approach then and there. But just in case anybody might have thought Mr Ellis was not doing his job, Mr Rice wrote two astonishing sentences: 'The headmaster is sincerely [*i.e.* he was not faking] concerned about these problems and in fact he was recently absent due to nervous depression and worry.' And again, in a sentence that contains the only reference to Mrs Walker's criticisms and campaign: 'Although accepting the role of head teacher he has been too much influenced by different points of view among his staff some of whom have actively opposed him and his philosophy of education.' If a 'not' were inserted after 'although', the sentence would appear to have no less meaning.

It is possible that those sentences were never meant to be taken literally, that they constituted a sort of coded storm signal which Mr Rice believed would be correctly interpreted by those who read them. If so, Mr Rice was sadly mistaken; neither Miss Burgess nor Dr Birchenough came back and said, 'Mr Rice, what are you really trying to say about this school?' Mr Rice then went on to make three proposals: a staff meeting the following term to discuss educational policy at which he would be present; more money for more equipment; and a full-time unit run by a teacher/psychotherapist. Then he concluded: 'I am concerned that standards of both behaviour and attainment have fallen in the junior school. I feel that every support must be given at this stage to the headmaster and staff to boost morale and re-establish good standards and discipline.'

Mr Rice had made some criticisms, however muted; he had made some proposals, however inadequate; surely he and Mr Ellis and the staff could be left alone now to establish friendly and 'supportive' relations with one another? Whether or not Mr Rice had that precise thought in mind, his reaction to the request for a meeting with him at the end of the month by a small group of managers certainly suggested something of the sort. Besides, quite correctly, insisting that the chairman of managers be present, he brought along his predecessor in the job, Mr Buxton, and the divisional and deputy divisional officer, together with a note-taker. The tenor of their advice to the managers was at all costs not to do anything, and certainly not before Christmas by which time Mr Ellis would have had a year to prove himself. The only concrete reason given – by Mr Buxton – was the fear of an explosion by the politically volatile Islington teachers, particularly if there were seen to be any trouble in a school where Mrs McColgan was teaching. We shall have more to say about that in the next chapter. In the meantime, the managers must have been asking themselves what more they had to do in order to get their own and the widespread concern about the school taken seriously.

Mr Rice's second report, eight months later, was made at Mr Hinds's direct request in March 1975, and was rather fuller than the first. It was based, so he insisted at the inquiry, not just on an unannounced visit he made to the school on 4 March, but also on his continuous observation of the school and his various discussions with the staff. It was divided up into subject headings and followed the format which appeared to be generally typical of inspectors' reports – namely, a description of what was observed which might or might not be followed by a comment. Thus, on mathematics: 'This subject is taught in all classes but there seems to be little indication of a clear development of skills through the school. Greater co-ordination and setting of objectives is needed.' On art and music: 'There is little evidence of any co-ordinated effort in these subjects except for individual enthusiasm on the part of a few teachers.' On games and physical education: 'The school is involved in a fair amount of physical activity, particularly competitive games such as netball and football. No gymnastic activity or apparatus work has been observed in the school.' Similar remarks were made about reading standards, social education and religious education.

On school organisation and the co-operative teaching scheme, Mr Rice became a little bolder, but was careful to put the judgement into the words of Mr Ellis: 'The headmaster admits that this has not proved successful as there has been too little structure involved in the curriculum and the children have been left to their own devices.' Mr Rice added some brief general comments about parental lack of confidence, falling numbers and behavioural problems, but concluded, 'With the smaller numbers and very generous staffing ratio there is now much greater control and a quieter atmosphere throughout the school. It is estimated that a realistic roll for the junior school next year will be 125–130 children' (100 fewer than a year earlier). There were no recommendations for action.

On the basis of that, Mr Hinds certainly had no justification for telling the teachers, as he did four months later in July, that the report showed that there was nothing educationally wrong with the school. But if those whose job it was at the time to decide what to do – Mr Pape, Dr Birchenough and Mr Hinds, for example – had only that report to go on, they were grossly under-informed. There was no indication of the extent of the failure of the co-operative teaching scheme, of the degree of breakdown between teachers and managers at the beginning of the September term, of Miss Hart's renewed complaints about interruptions to the teaching in her infant school.

The options before them were: to order a full inspection; to order a visitation; or to leave things basically as they were. A full inspection would have meant a team of inspectors going into the school for a week, sitting in on every class, talking to teachers and children, going over their conclusions with the head and staff, and then writing a lengthy report. A visitation meant the mixture as before, but less of everything, and without the formal status of a full inspection. Following Mrs Page's approach to Mr Rice in January, the inspectors had already considered a full inspection but rejected it, partly on the grounds that, being the ultimate sanction, it left nothing to build upon. So the decision was to leave it to Mr Rice to keep a close watching-brief on the school, with the recommendation (which he failed properly to carry out) to get a number of subject inspectors in to advise on particular points. In restrospect, it was perhaps a mistake on Dr Birchenough's part not to have sent in a couple of more senior inspectors to provide a check on Mr Rice's impressions.

More worrying, though, than all that is the general style of the report. There does not appear to be anything in it which an intelligent layman, properly briefed, could not have found and written for himself after a day in the school. Mr Rice's comments were all based on observation – what was or was not the case –

unsupported by any clear notion of values – what ought or ought not to have been the case – still less any hierarchy of values (how important was it that visits to the Norfolk coast were not 'developed in school to provide an academic framework', whatever that may mean?)

Take again what Mr Rice had to say about mathematics. Supposing, instead of writing 'but there seems little indication of a clear development of skills throughout the school', he had put 'but on current showing few pupils are likely to reach the standard that will be expected of them when they go up to secondary school'. Now that would provide a benchmark against which to measure the efficiency of the teaching in the school – a vague and probably crude benchmark, but one that someone of Mr Rice's experience ought to have been able to handle. There might have been, for the sake of argument, some pupils for whom that would not have been 'suitable', whose 'requirements' might have been different. But there is no evidence that Mr Rice had any such notion in the back of his mind when observing the school; instead he appeared to content himself with throwing the ball back at the staff of the school. 'Greater . . . setting of objectives is needed.'

All in all, on the basis of Mr Rice's report, if the children in a school could be observed to be happily occupied, and the teaching controlled and planned, then there would be little cause for concern. The same blandness could be detected in the much fuller reports based on visits carried out by teams of inspectors in September and October of that year, just prior to the opening of the inquiry. As with Mr Rice's reports, descriptions take the place of value-judgements, or at best imply their own. In one of the reports, under the heading *Standards*, the first sentence reads, 'There is no agreed system of recording children's progress' – as though that were a criticism of the school and not of the authority.

The first visit, which was intended to be a full inspection, took place during the week beginning 22 September with a team led by Mr Pape. The staff went on strike, which meant that they were not available to talk and comment about their work; under those circumstances, the inspectorate decided that it could not grace its visit with the title of full inspection. More than that, 'the inspector-in-charge did not feel he should depart from the normal courtesies so far as to open the files of the headmaster or examine the contents of the teachers' or *children*'s desks' (our italics). However, the team evidently did see enough to produce some pretty damning statements, such as 'the upstairs hall was indescribably bitty with a confusion of drama apparatus and library shelves, a

94

portable coat-hanger, a piano and two or three bedraggled items of display'.

Apart from that, the most trenchant criticisms were attributed to individual inspectors and put between inverted commas. Thus, an art inspector: 'The art room in which I taught for two afternoons is a barren desert. ... A working atmosphere in a school is brought about by the thought, care and pride which is put into the enrichment of the child's environment. Here the school has little to offer.' And a primary inspector's description of a classroom: 'A search of the classroom produced a good stock of miscellaneous papers and a small badly damaged collection of books forming a "library". Under the tables and around the room were plastic trays holding exercise books, paper and a few copies of a maths textbook. There was nothing else usable. The room was spacious, the furniture was plentiful and in good repair, although the cupboards lacked shelves. There was a sink, an old typewriter, a few cards pinned to the walls. There were no readers, no apparatus, no art materials and none of the valuable and common stimulating equipment that a primary classroom usually holds.' The conclusion of that report, which was signed by Dr Birchenough, was that 'the condition of the school as presented to the inspectors during their visit to it is such as to warrant a full inspection of it at the earliest opportunity'.

The report of the second inspection added little to the first apart from comments by the staff and Mr Ellis of the sort which were expanded at greater length in the inquiry. What was staggering, however, was the extraordinary feebleness of the conclusion, which was again signed by Dr Birchenough. Clearly, he could not get away with calling for a full inspection a second time. But, as the following final passage shows, there was nothing else he could do instead:

When all account is taken of the quite abnormal circumstances of the inspection, they found cause for concern in it which demanded fuller examination and explanation. It was remarked that head and assistant teachers did not speak of each other's qualities to the inspectors. There is perhaps no clear lead in the school – the head may not want to lead. The fervour of some staff may have led inexperienced teachers out of their pedagogical depth. For some there is such a conviction in their beliefs and practices that they are perhaps not open to persuasion upon them. The question remains, how much are they in the right and how much in error and what is the true level of their achievements and their failures and what might they be prepared to do about it? The inspectors have submitted their findings as the outcome of a most difficult assessment exercise and with all the qualifications inherent in the exceptional circumstances. They are not in a position to offer a final judgement.

A full inspection normally depended on the co-operation of the staff. In this case, the inspectors, when that co-operation was not forthcoming, appeared to have nothing to fall back on and, to all intents and purposes, gave up.

That brings us back to the question with which we started the chapter: who is entitled to make a final judgement? The managers were not equipped to, the HMIs didn't want to – they studiously kept William Tyndale at arm's, not to say barge-pole's, length – and now Dr Birchenough and his troops were 'not in a position to'. As a result of the inquiry, Dr Birchenough planned to increase the number of primary inspectors and to step up the number of planned full inspections to around ten a year (six years previously these were running at about five a year). He also intended to try to persuade teachers to accept some form of attainment testing – to provide the criteria of efficiency that were so conspicuously lacking at William Tyndale. But on the evidence of these reports, that would involve a truly agonising reappraisal of the inspectors' role.

9. The Union's not their Leader

Throughout the story of William Tyndale there was a spectre haunting the officers and members of the ILEA: the spectre of London teachers in revolt. Would the Islington teachers rise? If so, would they be joined by their only slightly less militant neighbours, the Hackney teachers? Time and again, during the events and after them, fear of teachers' reactions was put forward as the reason or the pretext for the authority's inaction – but always in subdued tones, off the record, not to be repeated, and so on. By a nice piece of legal bargaining, the issue was even kept well in the background during the inquiry. Mr Ellis and his colleagues, for reasons we shall go into, wanted the advice they had received from the NUT kept secret on the grounds that, having come from the union's legal department, it was 'privileged'. Mr Auld accepted; it transpired afterwards that all questions of teacher politics were to be kept firmly in the background. And yet in many respects those questions were absolutely central. Mr Ellis and his colleagues were all members of the National Union of Teachers, which is the most powerful pressure group in the world of education. Had the union espoused their cause, the outcome might have been very different. In fact, by at first doing nothing and then refusing to support the teachers' strike action, the union rendered a signal service to the ILEA. Few senior members or officers of the NUT had much sympathy for the William Tyndale teachers and several of them, including some who were also prominent in the Islington branch (called confusingly but inaccurately the North London Teachers' Association), were of the opinion that the authority should have acted much sooner. But, they would always add, they understood why the authority had preferred not to take any action during that summer of 1974.

The teachers were restless during that summer, for straightforward economic reasons. They were simply one of a large number of groups of employees – dustmen, nurses, civil servants, and so on – whose relative standard of living was dropping behind that of the private sector during the boom years of the sixties and early seventies. Londoners were particularly badly hit, and among Londoners, teachers. Being members of an exceptionally mobile profession, they rarely qualified for council housing. London house prices were rocketing far more sharply than in the provinces, and rented accommodation was becoming scarcer and scarcer. By the early 1970s a young married teacher whose wife had stopped working to start a family could be a lot worse off than, say, a dustman who was one of two or three earners sharing a council flat; teachers had become part of the new white-collar poor.

It would be suprising if all that had not had a direct effect on London's schools. We have already seen in Chapter 6 how it may have affected the number and quality of applicants for Mr Ellis's job; fewer teachers of the right calibre were willing to work in London. It also had the effect of driving many of those who were teaching in London to adopt increasingly militant trade union tactics in support of their claims for a higher London Allowance. Throughout the early 1970s, their campaign, with its protests, demonstrations and one-day unofficial stoppages, brought a degree of bitterness and bad feeling into staffrooms which, in some cases, had the effect of driving even more good teachers away. This is not to say that the activists were worse teachers than the non-activists. The difference was between those who put the interests of the children before those of the profession, and those who did not; and those who put the children first were certainly likely to contain a higher proportion of committed teachers, and possibly of good ones as well. This clash between professionalism and trade unionism had affected William Tyndale Mr Head, the headteacher who had preceded Mr Ellis there, had been highly thought of as a classroom teacher – 'like all good teachers, he had a rather idiosyncratic teaching style' as one colleague of his put it – and had carried his commitment with him to William Tyndale. The unrest in the staffroom and Mr Head's departure in 1973 to another headship in rural Oxfordshire could well be laid at the door of the London schools campaign.

The unresolved contradiction between trade union politics and the attitudes of a professional association is the cross that the main teachers' union, the National Union of Teachers – and those who have had dealings with it – have had to bear since the union's inception. It was from the very start in the uncomfortable position of using 'professional' arguments – the best way of teaching – to buttress a case that was essentially a trade union one: payment by results meant low pay for teachers. Similarly, the union had frequently resorted to standard trade union tactics in pursuit of goals, such as the reduction of class sizes, that appeared, superficially at least, to be more akin to the aims of a professional association. This dual concern of the union had led to the paradox of young radical teachers, whose commitment in other spheres to democratic procedures and political accountability might have led them to promote the accountability of teachers to the community, lining up behind the sacred cow of autonomy in the classroom.

On most issues, the union leadership and its members were at one. The majority of NUT members consisted of primary school teachers most of whom were female and professionally and politically conservative. By a curious irony, this membership was on the whole well enough represented by a leadership dominated by secondary school headmasters, some of whom were avowed members of the Communist Party and most of whom, including the communists, were conservative on professional matters. But this was not true for a fringe group of young teachers who had been radicalised by their economic situation, the propaganda of the International Socialists and what they saw as the possibilities inherent in teaching for changing society. Most of these tended to be in London and, unlike the mass of the membership, tended to regard the leadership as being too professionally oriented to be effective trade unionists and too conservative to be effective professional reformers.

When Mr Ellis and his colleagues needed help, they first turned to their local association, the NLTA, whom they knew to be on the same sort of radical wavelength as themselves, rather to the union headquarters in Hamilton House or its inner London regional official. True, they did approach the regional official on a trivial point as early as June 1974, but it was not until about a year later that full contact was established, with the official going into the school and relaying the advice of the union's educational or legal departments. Despite warnings that had been dropped into the ears of both the general secretary and the head of the education department by a local headteacher earlier in 1975, only one senior union official apparently had direct contact with the teachers, and that was the union solicitor at meetings on 6 August and 17 September (the second one was mainly to do with an action that Mr Ellis was bringing against the *Evening News*). It was on those occasions that the advice was given which was to be considered 'privileged' at the enquiry. But there is little doubt that the whole tenor of the union's advice was the same: namely, that the teachers had no grounds on which to resist the authority's proposal for a full inspection preceding the inquiry and that any attempts by them to do so by, for example, going on strike would not only put the teachers in the position of breaking the law but also put them in breach of union rules.

The law was Clause 4 of Section 77 of the 1944 Act which states: 'If any person obstructs any person authorised to make an inspection in pursuance of the provisions of this section in the execution of his duty, he shall be liable on summary conviction to a fine not exceeding twenty pounds, or, in the case of a second or subsequent conviction, to a fine not exceeding fifty pounds or to imprisonment for a term not exceeding three months or to both such imprisonment and such fine.' The union rule in question was No. 8 in the subsection on the constitution in the 1975 annual report: 'No constituent association or division of the union, or members thereof, shall organise or engage in a strike or industrial action without prior approval of the Executive.'

The teachers did not accept the advice they received from their union; indeed, at one point, Dr Briault at least got the impression from the teachers that their union had told them it would be all right for them to go on strike. It could be, of course, that with the ILEA so fearful of what the teachers might do, it would not have taken much to give Dr Briault that impression anyway. But if the teachers did not like the advice itself, they probably liked even less the tone in which it was apparently given. The union's position, as put to us by a senior official, was: 'If you've got a dispute with your managers or the authority, you come to us first – you don't go off and present us with a *fait accompli*.' The same official complained to us in so many words that the teachers had never gone along for an informal chat with anybody at Hamilton House.

The reason was that Mr Ellis and his colleagues were interested in using not so much the technical services of the union, which was what Hamilton House could offer them, but the pressure of numbers which only the members could bring to bear – and for that, they had to work through the NLTA. And if the NLTA wanted to widen the dispute still farther, they would have to work through the Inner London Teachers' Association (ILTA); in fact, as it turned out, it was at that level that Hamilton House blocked the attempt by the William Tyndale teachers to put a match to the tinder which the NUT knew only too well was lying around.

Membership of the NLTA was running at a little over 1,000; fewer than half of those voted in elections for officers, and fewer than one-tenth would turn up to meetings at any one time. Two main factions contested the leadership: a Broad Left coalition, which mainly included anybody not to the left of the Communist Party, and Rank and File, a grassroots movement of teachers heavily influenced by the International Socialists. At the time of the dispute, the Broad Left was in power, but the very existence of the rival factions meant that there was continual competition for the title of 'most militant'. Many of the extremists in the association were young secondary school teachers whose jobs, by their very nature, did not provide the outlets for radical professional experimentation that primary school teachers enjoyed. *Rank and File*, the newsheet of the movement, was quick to compare William Tyndale with Risinghill, the Islington comprehensive run by Michael Duane which had been closed in 1965 by the authority.

Prior to William Tyndale, and apart from the London teachers' campaign, the issue which had perhaps most exercised the NLTA was that of Mrs McColgan. In 1969, along with three other teachers from Highbury Quadrant, Mrs McColgan was in dispute with her headteacher and the ILEA. On the whole, the other teachers found other satisfactory jobs – one of them was teaching at Canonbury Junior School, next door to William Tyndale. Mrs McColgan and the authority, however, continued to be in dispute, and she was only able to get a job at Hungerford Infants School, where she taught until June 1971, on the understanding that she would not have tenure. Whatever the respective merits of Mrs McColgan's and the authority's cases – the details are not relevant here – the whole affair provided a splendid 'teachers' rights' case for the NLTA to take up. That was one reason why the ILEA probably breathed a sigh of relief when Mrs McColgan was taken on at William Tyndale with a normal contract; but it also meant that William Tyndale had, so to speak, a hot line to the NLTA.

Back in the summer of 1974, the William Tyndale staff had brought the activities of Mrs Walker to the attention of the association and in October they received a letter of general support from the association's general purposes committee. But it was not until its meeting of 2 June 1975 that the association began to influence the course of events. At that meeting, attended by sixty-one members, the following motion, proposed by the staff of the school, was approved:

(a) NLTA condemns the vicious campaign over the last thirteen months against the staff of the William Tyndale Junior School.
(b) The falling roll resulting from this campaign has serious implications for the staff. We therefore call upon NLTA members in neighbouring schools to oppose admission to their schools of children from William Tyndale Junior and Infant Schools.

(c) We call on the NUT legal department to take action to defend the teachers under attack.

That motion incensed a number of the school's managers who, it will be remembered, had just passed a resolution themselves calling on the ILEA to do something about the declining numbers of children in the school. They felt that the motion was a direct threat to the rights of parents to send their children to the school of their choice. However, many teachers who might, like the managers, have been worried about the long-term implications of the association's stand, supported it not so much for the sake of the staff as for the sake of the school. If the rapid decline in numbers continued the closure of the school would be inevitable and they, like Mrs Page for example, felt that would do nobody any good.

At the next monthly meeting, the association supported the staff's stand in refusing to allow managers into the school during working hours. Then, on 8 September, after the authority's decision to inspect the school, the association passed another motion, again put forward by the William Tyndale staff, which called for, among others, the following steps:

(a) The ILTA to demand immediately from the ILEA that the primary purpose of an inquiry which might take place shall be a full investigation of the origin and purpose of the political attacks made on the William Tyndale Junior School . . .

(c) That the ILTA demand that no inspection of the William Tyndale School should precede the necessary investigation into the political allegations which have been made . . . .

This was an attempt, in other words, to limit the scope of the inquiry and to prevent any prior inspection of the school. Events now moved rapidly. The council of the ILTA declined to support the teachers, saying 'that while the Council recognised the anxiety of the members of William Tyndale School, it was of the view that the members should co-operate fully with the inspection, confident in the knowledge that their interests would be safeguarded by the union'. The education committee of the NUT endorsed that opinion on 19 September, and put through an urgent report to the executive the next day, Saturday 20 September. By this time the union knew that the teachers were planning to strike from the following Monday, the day the inspection was due to start, and the general secretary of the union formally wrote to the teachers to advise them that, if they went on strike, they would be in breach of union rules.

In the meantime, Mr Ellis and his colleagues had collected the necessary fifty signatures to request a special general meeting of the NLTA on 24 September, in order to get the association's support for 'the action that members of William Tyndale Junior School have taken in opposition to the full general inspection imposed on the school by the ILEA'. The association's general purposes committee, which had up to now fully supported the William Tyndale teachers, changed its tune. Doubtless bearing in mind the attitude of the ILTA and of Hamilton House, it announced on 15 September that it could not support the motion proposed for the special meeting, mainly on the grounds that 'the authority is charged with the duty of providing education for the children in its area and has the right and duty of inspecting the establishments in which this education is being given'.

That meeting turned out to be crucial: if the NLTA were to support the striking teachers, both the authority and the union would be placed in a most awkward position. Nearly 200 people, twice as many as usual, turned up. Mr Ellis and Mr Haddow proposed their motion and then an amendment was put down by the association's executive which was tantamount to an expression of support for the William Tyndale staff on every point except that of strike action. The debate on that amendment was conducted in terms which highlighted once again the central dilemma of the union: trade unionism or professionalism. Curiously, the strongest pleas on both sides were put by secondary school teachers, Jeff Herford of Shelburne Girls' School arguing that they were a trade union first and last, and that the members' interests should therefore come before everything else; while on the other side Margaret Maden, headmistress of Islington Green Comprehensive, in a powerful speech which, according to many who were there, carried the day, said, 'We not only have legal obligations, but a moral one as well'. In the end, the amendment was carried by 110 votes to 77, and the ILEA was able to breathe again. If the outcome was indeed decided by Miss Maden, the irony could not have been lost on those present; only a few years earlier, Miss Maden had been one of the prominent and active members of Rank and File.

Most accounts of trade union machinations tend to leave the impression that they are rather parochial affairs, and this is no exception. It does give an indication, however, among other things, of the extent of the William Tyndale teachers' paranoia; practically every motion contained a reference to the 'political accusations' being made against them. It also shows the extent to which even the most militant branch of the union was not prepared to rock the educational boat; when it came to the crunch – whether or not to support the William Tyndale teachers in their unofficial strike – the NLTA was not prepared to declare war on Hamilton House and the educational establishment. But that in itself raises the question of whether the ILEA had not been too scared of the union from the beginning; if Mr Buxton had felt that he and the inspectors had a free rein, would he have tried so hard in July 1974 to dissuade the managers from taking any precipitate action? Without the ever-present, and perhaps unjustified, fear of what the NLTA might do, might Dr Birchenough six months later have recommended a full inspection? And if these things had happened, would that have been enough to prevent the school coming to the pass it did the following September? A number of London's inspectors had long been convinced that both primary and secondary schools were hotbeds of left-wing political activism; their convictions on this occasion may have led the whole inspectorate into error and, in effect, destroyed the school. The London schools campaign, by creating the sort of atmosphere in which those sort of beliefs could flourish, had perhaps more to answer for than it realised.

10. The 'Trial' of William Tyndale

Robin Auld, QC, was asked to conduct a public inquiry 'into the teaching, organisation and management of the William Tyndale Junior and Infant Schools, Islington, London, N1, and thereafter to report' to Mr Hinds. The leaders of the authority went into the inquiry, which began on 27 October 1975, like the volunteers of August 1914, confident that it would all be over by Christmas. The temporary teachers who were running the junior school had been told that they would be needed for about three weeks and – an even stronger indication of the authority's optimism – the ILEA had offered to pay virtually everybody's legal fees. As it turned out, there were some seventy hearings spanning fourteen weeks and over a hundred witnesses, all of which provided work, in one way or another, for around twenty lawyers.

The teachers, however, had prepared for a long war of attrition from the start. Determined to make a fight of it, they probably gained more than they lost by the refusal of the National Union of Teachers to represent them. For, into the breach, stepped the new Law Clinic of the University of Kent and the Clinic's radical university lecturer-lawyers already had considerable experience of *ad hoc* inquiry and tribunal proceedings. The Clinic's solicitor was Larry Grant, formerly legal officer of the National Council for Civil Liberties; the barrister he briefed was Stephen Sedley, a member of one of the few left-wing chambers of barristers in London and one of the most experienced lawyers at the inquiry. He had already made something of a name for himself at the Red Lion Square tribunal presided over by Lord Justice Scarman, and after this inquiry was over, was to make fleeting headlines when he flew out to Angola to take part in a jurists' commission at the time of the trial of the British mercenaries. Thus, he and Mr Grant had a better idea than the ILEA side of what to expect. For example, Mr Ellis and his colleagues produced for the inquiry something which they had consistently failed to put together for the parents, managers and inspectors: a comprehensive statement of what they were trying to achieve in the school.

The teachers' advisers realised, as nobody else appeared to have done, that if the style and length of the inquiry would be dictated to some extent by the mass of documents, approaching 500 in all, which had been submitted in evidence, it would be determined even more by the structure of the proceedings themselves. Mr Auld, had already headed a number of routine disciplinary inquiries for the ILEA and when, back in July 1975, the authority had first put forward the notion of an inquiry under an outside chairman, they had assumed that the various parties to the inquiry would be content to rely on Mr Auld to protect their legal rights. They had hoped that no other lawyers would be involved. And right up until the first few days of the hearings, they had expected that the barristers representing their own interests would be accepted by everybody else as being a sort of impartial counsel to the inquiry.

The assumption behind that – and behind the modern practice of appointing a 'counsel to the inquiry' even when it is presided over by a lawyer – is that the proceedings will be inquisitorial and not accusatorial. That is to say that Mr Auld, whose brief had been to report on the facts of the case, would have been acting like a continental *juge d'instruction*, whose task is to determine precisely what happened, rather than as a judge in a traditional British court who presides over a sort of gladiatorial contest between police and prisoner or plaintiff and defendant. A number of factors, however, combined to turn the proceedings into something that was in many important respects much closer to a trial than to an inquiry.

There was the layout and atmosphere of the inquiry room itself. Room 143 on the first floor of County Hall, a cold and impersonal room where both the education committee and more recently the schools subcommittee used to meet, had no dock. But with its dark oak panelling, raised dais at one end and tiered galleries at the other, it could well have served as a county assize court. In the well, divided by a central gangway, were three diagonal rows of tables at which sat the lawyers and, behind them, their clients. Teachers and managers were therefore facing one another as much as facing Mr Auld, who from the height of his dais presided like a judge, flanked by his two advisers, Dora Loftus, a retired Labour Party organiser, and George Carter, headteacher of a London comprehensive school. Both were members of the schools subcommittee and originally it had been intended that they should sit in judgement along with Mr Auld. However, in the end, the authority decided that responsibility for both the conduct of the proceedings and producing the final report would be that of the trained lawyer on his own. Apart from Mr Auld's advisers and the lawyers, almost the only people consistently present throughout the inquiry were, like prisoners in the dock, Mr Ellis and his colleagues, who were all on paid leave of absence.

More important, perhaps, was the refusal of all the parties to accept the impartiality of the authority and so allow the authority's counsel, Edward Davidson, to serve in any way as a counsel to the inquiry. Such a counsel would have been able, as a result of a great deal of preliminary sifting and elimination of irrelevant documents and witnesses, to present a skeleton outline to everybody right at the start of the proceedings. The barristers acting for the seven parties represented – the authority, the managers, Mr Ellis and his six colleagues, Mrs Chowles, Miss Hart and the infant school staff, the London borough of Islington and Mrs Walker – would then have known in advance what was to come and would not have needed to cross-examine every witness at such inordinate length.

As it was, the proceedings were made still longer by Mr Auld's insistence on accepting only spoken evidence – which meant that someone had to testify to the authenticity of every document, however trivial. The purpose of this rule was to avoid the inquiry being inundated with the written views of people who were not prepared to come along and back them. However, Mr Auld did abandon after some weeks a rule which was clearly proving a great time-waster – namely, that every witness should read out in full the summary of his evidence, often amounting to many thousands of words, which was already being circulated in writing.

The first witness was Mr Rice. His treatment by the other parties set the pattern of the inquiry. It became clear at once that neither the managers nor the teachers were going to accept the ILEA inspectors as impartial experts and that their behaviour and their opinions would be challenged exhaustively by both groups. Mr Rice was treated in cross-examination as though he were a defendant in the dock; and it was clear that the authority, whatever its earlier hopes, would have to fight for its reputation like everyone else.

The inspectorate had already, on the eve of the proceedings, begun to suspect that it was being left to carry the can for the rest of the ILEA officer corps. Harried to the point of exhaustion by the seven counsel who took him over the same ground in turn seeking different answers, Mr Rice gave them; and drew the taunt that he would say whatever people wanted to hear. Confused and fearful for his personal position, he appeared in the end to be saying that he and, as far as he knew, everyone else in the authority was virtually powerless to act in the William Tyndale situation; and that his own hesitant views on its urgencies at crucial times were either misunderstood by his superiors or failed to move them. Treated by the opposition rather as though he were the spokesman for the whole authority, Mr Rice knew that neither Mr Wales, by now retired, nor Dr Briault, who carried the ultimate responsibility for Mr Wales's actions, was going to appear and let his resentment at their absence boil over. 'I should not be placed in the position of having to deal with that question,' he protested. 'I am being asked about matters which are the responsibility of officers who are equipped to deal with them.'

Dr Birchenough echoed more coherently Mr Rice's view of the inspectorate's impotence, emphasising that it was expected to support and to persuade rather than to judge or to admonish. But Mr Pape and Mr Buxton, whose memories went back to an older tradition of the inspectorate, were, in their different ways, very much tougher; some of the William Tyndale teachers, Mr Pape went so far as to say, had avoided the chores of teaching. At ease, obviously enjoying the oportunity to display his expertise, he expounded and vigorously defended informal teaching methods and the value of letting children choose; the approach should not be judged by what had happened at William Tyndale, he insisted. Mr Buxton, whose antipathy towards County Hall's top brass had never been hidden from his colleagues, was fiercely loyal to his branch: he did not mention that he had tried himself to alert Dr Birchenough to the seriousness of the situation. But he challenged truculently Mr Davidson's claim to represent him, making it clear that he did not believe that the interests of the authority were identical with those of its officers.

The ILEA's star witness was Mr Hinds. If Mr Rice had appeared pitiably weak, Mr Hinds cut a still sorrier figure in his attempts to be strong. He answered awkward questions with sweeping generalities interlaced with assorted metaphors: people had wanted him to wear hobnailed boots when he felt ballet shoes more appropriate; his arm had been 'forced right up my back'. Asked to explain his lack of action, his hopes that the conflict would be resolved and the apparent powerlessness of the ILEA's control mechanisms, he returned time and again to a basic theme: he and the authority – he spoke much of the time as though he personified it – relied on 'groups of adults behaving in a fair and civilised manner in accordance with their own consciences'. It was the basis of the whole English school system, he claimed approvingly. He implied that, while both he and the authority had behaved throughout in a suitably grown-up way, they had been sadly let down by the immature conduct of those who were now criticising him. But Mr Hinds had, in the end, to come down to the specific questions that counsel were asking and here he was shown no mercy. When he dismissed a phrase in a record of a conversation as an error on the part of his personal assistant, Mr Auld insisted on calling the young woman to testify (she stood firmly by her version). But Mr Hinds was determined to preserve the image of himself as the man at the top of London's educational ladder – at least insofar as schools were concerned. This meant that he could not shelter behind the absent figure of Sir Ashley Bramall. Passing references to Sir Ashley in correspondence cited in evidence hinted that from time to time the ILEA leader had been informed or consulted about aspects of the situation. Mr Hinds did not refer to him and so made certain that if any political head should, in the end, roll, it would be his own – as indeed it was.

All in all, Mr Hinds had a rough ride. He was brought back time and again to his statement that on the basis of Mr Rice's report he had concluded that the school was no worse than any other inner London school. After the barristers had finished, Mr Auld moved in.

At the meeting with the teachers in July 1975, the chairman asked, had Mr Hinds not said that the school was satisfactory?

Hinds: I may well have said words to the effect that it was as satisfactory on balance as any London primary school having regard to the particular situation of the school.

What circumstances did you have in mind?

Hinds: First, that there was a comparatively recently appointed head; secondly, that no one else except the deputy had been long in the school; and thirdly, that it was in a disadvantaged area, and the accommodation tight by modern standards. I should say, however, that the building was not excessively bad or small by comparison with hundreds of other ILEA primary schools. A large number of our 840 primary schools go back to the beginning of the century.

It was two days before you were going to propose a full inspection and an inquiry into the school, was it not?

Hinds: I was referring to Mr Rice's report . . .

Why should you be referring back to Mr Rice's views in March? Was it your view in July that the school was satisfactory on balance?

Hinds: By July the school was far from satisfactory but I had no more up-to-date knowledge of the actual work of the school.

The admission went oddly with Mr Hinds's earlier claims that arriving at his office at County Hall at 8.30 a.m. and staying until the early hours, he was able to keep tabs on all the authority's schools and take effective action as and when necessary. He had boasted of the 'massive flow' of information that came to him.

What had changed, Mr Auld wanted to know, in the situation two days later when he decided on an inquiry? Mr Hinds went back to his favourite track.

Hinds: What had happened was the information that came to me from various sources and discussions between those groups of adults, or some of those groups, on whose relationships depend a great deal of what is of value in the English educational system.

You were asked to say if it was a fair statement that there was nothing wrong with the school.

Hinds: I think that was my state of mind on 2 July that there was nothing particularly wrong.

The assessment of a school's academic achievement, he added, was a job for the highly paid professionals, and not for him. He had considered the reports with his advisers having regard to what he knew of the background. 'What they did not add up to was a situation in which aggressive intervention would be justified or helpful. There was a note from the education officer to myself roughly supporting that view.'

Did Mr Rice's report of March 1975 justify you in saying there was nothing wrong educationally with the school?

Hinds: It did not justify me in doing more than asking Mr Rice to pay regular visits. I am not competent to make educational judgements. That is why I employ inspectors and pay them very large salaries.

A nice point – but the inspectorate had got there first. Mr Rice had already told the inquiry that while the view that Mr Hinds had expressed to the teachers might be 'tenable', it was not Mr Rice's; and that it was certainly not a correct interpretation of what he had reported. Mr Hinds had again allowed himself to be led into a trap. Nobody was asking him to make an educational judgement. What was at issue was whether he had competently judged the meaning of the advice given by one of the men to whom he paid those very large salaries.

The managers were represented by Tessa Moorhouse, who had trained as an educational psychologist before going to the Bar. Like Mr Sedley, she had been briefed by a left-wing solicitor; Bruce Douglas-Mann, MP, solicitor for the managers, had close links with the NCCL. But Mrs Moorhouse lacked Mr Sedley's experience and skill and frequently found that she was irritating Mr Auld no less than the witnesses she was questioning.

However, she had a much more daunting task: to keep her clients' distance from Mrs Walker's extremism but at the same time to justify the managers' actions. Thus Mrs Moorhouse emphasised, sometimes to the point of tedium, that it was no part of her case that progressive education had failed at William Tyndale. 'The managers are saying that the children are not taught at all,' she insisted. But despite all her efforts to restrict the debate to that one apparently straightforward issue of fact, the arguments at the inquiry ranged much wider. John Williams, Mrs Walker's counsel, who confessed to us halfway through the inquiry that he had had to learn about the educational issues while he was on his feet, had started out by pressing the attack on free choice methods. Mr Pape's eager acceptance of the challenge had set in train the broad debate which at one point seemed to be extending to the question of whether it had been wise to drop the 11-plus. The teachers' lawyers, aware above all that their clients' best chance lay in taking on the mantle of martyrs to the progressive cause, assiduously stoked the argument.

But Mrs Moorhouse also had to justify the pressure tactics of the managers, particularly those who had acted independently of the main managing body. As always, it was a good deal harder to defend than to attack; and Mr Auld's clearly demonstrated disapproval of some of her client's actions made it very heavy going. With Mrs Hoodless, as he already had with Mr Hinds, Mr Auld took over the questioning. Already pushed by Mr Davidson for the ILEA to explain why she had kept the managers as a whole in ignorance of the meetings with Mr Hinds or of the petition, Mrs Hoodless found herself forced into a corner by a far tougher Mr Auld. Couldn't she have called a special meeting? What part had she thought the rest of the managers should be playing? Did she expect Mr Hinds to act without referring to the full managing body? If she didn't want Mr Haddow or Mr Ellis to know about it, couldn't she have spoken to the other managers without them? In the end she agreed that with hindsight it would have been better to have brought the whole managing body in from the start. Mr Auld drove the point home: 'They were left out of it for a very long time. Why weren't they informed?' Mrs Hoodless could only say that to keep everyone informed would have taken 'a good deal of hard work'.

On top of this, not all the managers who gave evidence were willing to help Mrs Moorhouse's defence of the actions of Mrs Hoodless and her friends. Miss Morris, a Conservative nominee, said that she had felt shut out. John Bolland, the representative of the London Institute of Education, said that he found himself in conflict with those who were involved in the petition. Mr Tennant, at pains to present himself as a statesmanlike moderate, refrained from overt criticism but managed to dissociate himself from the group very effectively.

The parents, for whom special evening sittings had been arranged at a teachers' centre in Islington, were expected to be the managers' strongest card. The voice of the grassroots was, as Mr Auld was to note in passing in his report, a very divided voice. Held in a small, packed lecture room, the Islington sessions brought home the gulf between the actors in the conflict and most of those upon whom or on whose behalf they had acted. The basic ground rules of the inquiry, the constraints imposed by law, custom and practice on both manner and matter, had been accepted from the start by all those involved in the proceedings at County Hall, apart from one of the teachers, Stevie Richards, who resigned her job and abandoned the proceedings because, as she said, she 'could not relate' to what was going on around her. Like her, many of the working-class parents at the Islington hearings were unable to relate the inquiry proceedings to the strongly emotive reality of what had happened to their school. They could not accept that the lawyers were entitled to ask them what they saw as insulting questions or to impugn their judgement or veracity: some reacted with shouts or oaths, and one man was barely restrained from beating up Mr Sedley. Others were clearly out of their depth; and it was curiously affecting to hear adults stoutly praise their own traditional schooling after they had stumbled painfully through the task of reading out their own statements. Not all the parents were, however, working class or anti-Ellis: apart from the infant parents, they appeared to be divided almost equally between supporters and critics, with roughly the same broad social mix in each group.

Mr Ellis, who came at last, after Christmas, to face the questioners, was a very different figure from the man who had hit out angrily at his accusers in front of the TV cameras during the strike. Some of those who had been his most contemptuous critics earlier felt that he had matured during the inquiry, and continued to do so on the witness stand. For five weeks Mr Ellis had been hearing himself discussed at inordinate length and described in a variety of ways: weak, amiable, evasive, brilliant, rude, visionary, chaotic, muddled, caring. He had heard some of his most determined opponents declare how likeable and unassuming he was, and pay tribute to his own high quality as a teacher. Hearing his actions and character, and that of his enemies too, repeatedly picked over had produced a dual effect: it had enabled him to distance himself from his fears and resentments, and to examine critically the myth of the man. Fascinated increasingly by the dynamics of the inquiry, he lost his pessimistic scepticism. By the time Mr Ellis mounted the stand, he no longer talked as though the inquiry were wholly a charade; he had become, for the moment, an insider, intent on playing the game well.

The teachers were no longer the only ones on the defensive; their critics had been badly marked and there was certainly no hint in Mr Ellis's manner of the intolerant visionary or the defiant underdog. The prominent place which educational philosophies and technical questions had come to play in the battle gave him an enormous advantage. Mr Ellis was no longer simply a man defending his reputation and his career: he was now in the position of an expert witness, able to help Mr Auld understand what was involved in educational controversies.

He and his lawyers made the most of it: Mr Ellis on free choice Mr Ellis on backward children, on parents and their aspirations, on staffroom democracy, on what a headteacher should expect from his managers, on educating children for the year 2000, on the limitations of formal teaching. For the best part of two weeks on the witness stand he played the questions cooly and authoritatively, appearing tolerant rather than weak, and tossing out well-turned aphorisms at every chance. In the process he laughed off suggestions that he could be persuaded to share his pay in the name of egalitarianism, and assured the inquiry that, firm democrat that he was, he knew how to run a staffroom democracy so as to keep it safe for the headteacher. Only Mr Williams for Mrs Walker managed early on to shake him. Mr Ellis had told him that, as the teachers got used to working together, the need for meetings of the staff committee grew progressively less and it just withered away. Mr Williams pounced: 'This phrase, withering away, it's a curious choice of words, isn't it?' Mr Ellis managed to look surprised. Mr Auld, clearly unfamiliar with classic Marxist texts, looked impatient.

Whereas, as the inquiry had worn tediously on, Mr Ellis had taken to going out for an occasional smoke, Mr Haddow stayed closely following the proceedings the whole time. As a witness, he cut a less engaging figure than his headteacher. Sitting with his body hunched but with his head bent rigidly back so that the blond bearded chin jutted, his manner was a good deal sharper. It seemed not so much aggressive, as faintly insolent; suggesting that he was recognising the *de facto* status of his questioners rather than the legitimacy of the system they represented. Again it was Mr Williams who all but broke through the veneer of confidence: he had Mr Haddow replying in defiant monosyllables. Mr Auld, who had appeared deeply interested in Mr Ellis's pedagogic views, treated Mr Haddow with the same kindly curiosity. At one point, when Mr Haddow had given what appeared to be a damagingly lame reason for an action, Mr Auld suggested to him a more favourable explanation, for all the world as though he were Mr Haddow's own counsel. It seemed at that point as though the inquiry was going increasingly in favour of the teachers.

Mrs Walker, last of the witnesses, seemed to be doing her best to demonstrate the truth of Mr Ellis's complaint that attempts to discuss specifics with her tended to get lost in a sea of generalities. Mr Auld grew weary of her lengthy ruminations on the decline of standards in society at large and embarrassed by the ladylike reproofs she constantly addressed to counsel. She fought very hard to rebut the image of her, reinforced by Mr Williams's early tactics, as a crusader against progressive methods. Now, at the very end, came a cliff-hanging episode which destroyed much of her credibility. The final weeks of the inquiry had come increasingly to resemble the hammier examples of television courtroom drama: with an *in-camera* session, a violent outburst by Mrs Loftus against the lawyers' time-wasting, denunciations by the lawyers of attempts by spectators to influence witnesses, and an indignant complaint by Mr Williams that some of his opponents were laughing at him. On the last day of Mrs Walker's evidence, Mr Sedley tried to introduce the testimony of a forensic scientist, the kind of witness more commonly seen in murder trials. Now due to sum up, Mr Williams had to announce that a batch of important papers had just that minute turned up in Mrs Walker's garage. A solicitor rushed the papers to County Hall by taxi; the proceedings were adjourned overnight for counsel to study them. To everybody's surprise they turned out to include correspondence with Rhodes Boyson, a Conservative MP and untiring critic of progressive education.

In that correspondence was a document which Mrs Walker had been looking for in order to prove another point. She had taken the lot to her solicitor, who was compelled by the rules of his profession to disclose them all to the inquiry. The incident, and a renewed wave of argument, prolonged the inquiry by a couple more days. Mr Auld's last act was to thank the secretariat, mentioning that one of them had married during the course of the inquiry: the young lady was overcome with embarrassment at the sudden limelight, and so the inquiry ended, not with a bang but a simper. Mr Williams, who had been the most accusatorial of the advocates, complained in his final speech that it had followed the pattern, not of a public inquiry but of a criminal trial.

Whichever it was, it was certainly expensive.

The ILEA had agreed, at the last moment, to pay the costs of the parties – apart from Islington council – on a fixed scale of fees, £50 per day for a barrister for each party and a smaller sum for the solicitors. Together with Mr Auld's £100 per day and the cost of their own counsel, this concession meant that the authority in the end paid out a total of £50,000. The clerk to the greater London Council, which footed the bill out of its general administration funds, announced that a further £5,000 of expenditure had been incurred. But this clearly did not reflect the very substantial hidden costs of the operation. They included the salaries of the seven teachers (six after the departure of Miss Richards) on leave for nearly the whole of a school year, among whom were a head, a deputy and graded staff; the full-time use of a large secretariat headed by two senior ILEA staff for four months; and the involvement in preparation and testimony of a large number of other highly paid officers. If the authority had been able to present anyone with a bill of its true costs, it could scarcely have totalled much less than £100,000.

Epilogue

And When the Trial was over . . .

From the start of the inquiry, Mr Ellis and his colleagues were suspended on full pay and the school was kept running with some ninety pupils by a team of temporary teachers. There was some question of the teachers going back once the hearings were over, in February, but the authority had been told that, in that event, more parents would take their children away from the school. In any case, the authority was unwilling to make any decisions before receiving Mr Auld's report. Finally, Mr Ellis and his colleagues agreed to continue on paid leave of absence provided that the managers, who had been inclined to be punctilious about their legal obligations, also refrained from any action.

When the report finally arrived on Mr Hinds's desk, in July, Mr Auld was found to have scattered his shot fairly wide. He was not satisfied, as we have seen, that the education being provided at William Tyndale was either 'efficient' or 'suitable to the requirements' of the children under the terms of the 1944 Act. He laid the principal responsibility for the failure of the junior school and for the damaging role played by the staff in the disputes leading to the inquiry on Mr Ellis, though he described Mr Haddow as 'the main architect' of the troubles. The managers were criticised for their failure to use the procedures open to them, and certain of them were singled out for censure as having been involved in the 'harmful campaign' which accompanied the petition about the school. Mr Auld found that the ILEA had failed the school badly, mainly by not ordering a full inspection of it in 1974, and a number of officers were singled out for blame. But Mr Auld reserved some of his most severe strictures for the chairman of the schools subcommittee himself, Mr Hinds; he had not followed up the clear indication of serious trouble in the autumn of 1974; he had made a grave error of judgement in countenancing the organisation of the petition; and he had disregarded a warning that strife and disruption was likely to result from the 'petition and other activities' in hand.

The subcommitte made up its mind quickly. The junior and infant schools were to be combined into one establishment under Miss Hart. Dr Briault, the education officer, was to look into the possibility of taking disciplinary action against one or more of the ILEA officers. And in the autumn Mr Ellis and his colleagues were to go before a disciplinary tribunal to face charges based directly on Mr Auld's conclusions. All six were to be charged with indiscipline in connection with their strike twelve months earlier and the setting up of the alternative school; Mr Ellis was to be charged as well with misconduct in closing the school at the time of the strike and with inefficiency in allowing the school to deteriorate to the point it had reached in July 1974 and in general in not measuring up to his responsibilities as headmaster; and Mr Haddow was also to be charged with inefficiency in failing in the autumn term of 1974 properly to implement the co-operative teaching scheme for which he was responsible and in being the 'main architect of the beginning of the troubles at the Junior School, and . . . the driving force which caused Mr Ellis and the Junior School Staff to adopt the confrontation tactics leading to the final breakdown in relations in the Summer and Autumn of 1975'.

The five managers who were most severely criticised having decided to resign, there remained the question of Mr Hinds himself. At a meeting of the Labour group of education committee members, where the decisions were taken which were later ratified at the schools subcommittee meeting, Mr Hind's position as chief Labour whip on the GLC helped him obtain a massive vote of confidence from his own party members. Following that schools subcommittee meeting, however, the three ILEA members for Islington constituencies returned to face their local parties in the borough, all of which were extremely hostile to Mr Hinds. This was reported back to Mr Hinds and was thought to have been one of the determining factors in his decision – announced only four days after the vote of confidence in him – to resign as chairman of the schools subcommittee. Islington politicians, then, who had been complaining all along of their powerlessness to act in educational matters, would seem to have in the end influenced the course of events – though only when it was far too late for them to be of any help to William Tyndale.

The Auld Report

Unsurprisingly, as we saw in Chapter 10, Mr Auld adopted in his report an approach which revealed the logical mind of the jurist.

He sought to establish what had happened and what, as far as he could discover from the texts and the evidence, ought to have happened: his comments and value judgements, on the whole, flowed naturally from his comparison of the two. However, since all the main actors in the drama appeared before him in person, it was inevitable that personalities would influence his assessment; like any headmaster, Mr Auld appeared to have his teachers' pets. Mrs Chowles and Miss Hart could do no wrong, while Mr Tennant and Mrs Fairweather were criticised in ways which suggested that they had perhaps offended by their manner as much as in any other way. More importantly, the actions of Mrs Walker and the five managers who resigned were castigated in the strongest terms; but they might have been justified in retorting that, however 'disgraceful' or 'harmful' their behaviour, without it the situation in the school – which Mr Auld also roundly condemned – might well not have come to light.

On the substance of the report it is possible to have some sympathy with Mr Hinds's comment that it suffered from having been written by someone unfamiliar with the ways of the ILEA and of education. It is, though, another matter whether those ways ought to be protected by such an impenetrable barrier that not even Mr Auld could understand them, with all the resources of the inquiry at his disposal – let alone a common or garden taxpayer. Nevertheless, however uninformed they may have been, some of the ways in which Mr Auld set out the extent and limitations of the powers of those involved had implications far beyond the confines of Işlington, or even London.

Mr Auld made it quite clear that 'the headteacher is in effective control of the school, its aims, policies and methods of teaching'. But what if things go wrong? 'However unpalatable and whatever the practical, policy or political difficulties in choosing a solution [Mr Auld was thinking here of the 'regard that the authority quite properly has for the views of the teachers' professional associations in such matters'], if inefficient or unsuitable education is being provided at the school or insufficient regard is being paid to the wishes of parents of pupils at the school, the authority must do something about it.' That raised two questions. First, what precisely could the authority do about it? If all else failed, it could, he wrote, take over itself the control of the conduct and curriculum of the school; it could apply sanctions to the headteacher and the staff; it could close or reorganise the school.

The second question revealed the inadequacy of Mr Auld's approach and led him into deep waters: by what criteria can anyone judge whether a school is providing inefficient or unsuitable education? This was one of the many dilemmas the inspectors found themselves in and Mr Auld had some sympathy for them. 'Thus, if a headteacher is convinced that a particular educational policy or method is right for his school, and the district inspector is equally convinced that he is wrong, by what yardstick does the inspector judge and seek to advise the head that he is wrong?' By what indeed? Mr Auld had been gaily talking about 'efficiency' and 'suitability' but he was forced to recognise that, in practice – and London was no different in this respect from most other authorities – 'the authority has no policy:

(1) as to standards of attainment at which its primary schools should aim;
(2) as to the aims and objectives of the primary education being provided in its schools . . . ;
(3) as to the methods of teaching to be adopted in its schools.'

That was a damning indictment of an institution charged by law with educating London's children, but Mr Auld did not labour the point. For if to some extent it let the ILEA's inspectors off the hook, it also put Mr Auld himself in a rather difficult position. He was left with no yardstick by which to assess the performance of Mr Ellis and his colleagues; he had indeed precious little evidence as to their performance at all. They had scarcely been at the school long enough for any weight to be attached to comparisons between one year and another of children on the point of leaving the school (in fact, these showed William Tyndale to be on par with the average for inner London). Such reading tests as were done throughout the school were vitiated by the use of two different tests, the results of which proved to be mutually irreconcilable. Results of tests on the infants showed mainly that, by September 1974, the brighter children were being placed in schools other than William Tyndale. Moreover, Mr Ellis and his colleagues did not even bother much with keeping records of the children's progress – an omission which Mr Ellis admitted at the inquiry was probably a mistake. In fact, proper written records were, if anything, more important for an informal teacher than a formal one, as the children's freedom made it in other respects more difficult to keep track of them.

So in the end, to justify his assessment of the inefficiency and unsuitability of the education being provided at the school, Mr Auld was forced back on what he called 'the formidable weight of evidence'. Few people familiar with that evidence would want to quarrel with his verdict. The way he reached it, though, exposed him to the charge that for every question about powers and responsibilities that he answered, he raised – and left unanswered – another about what one might call the three 'A's: attainment, assessment and accountability.

By Way of Conclusion

The main ingredients of William Tyndale could be found all over the country: a staff with strong radical convictions, a weak headteacher, a dithering inspectorate, worried parents and a local education authority that did not know what it wanted of its primary schools. The mixture was common enough, but previously it had not been thought of as dangerously explosive. The *Zeitgeist*, however, had changed. Gone were the heady, spendthrift days of the 1960s when education and all the social services boomed, and books like Anthony Crosland's *The Future of Socialism* (actually published in 1956) could paint a rosy picture of a future full of beautiful people all happily caring for one another. In their place was the pessimism of the seventies, with their rapidly deteriorating cities and their visions of permanent economic decline inducing a desire to hang on to what was known and tangible, however irrational that might be. ('Catch a falling £ and put it in your pocket, Save it for a rainy day.') Combined with the fact that people's expectations of the welfare state had outrun their willingness to pay the consequent taxes, this meant, in education, a decline in the power of the teacher (the labour market was no longer running in his favour) and a concern for minimum standards. At its best, this could mean a concern for minimum standards for all children; at worst, it tended to be more selfishly inspired.

Attainment Mr Ellis, Mr Haddow and Mr Austin, if not all their followers, had a fairly clear idea of what they expected schools to do. Schools, for them, had a profound effect on children; the point was how to use that effect. Rather like the social workers referred to in Chapter 2, their main preoccupation was with the (largely false) dilemma of whether they, and schools, should be agents of social change or agents of social control. They wanted change and that was a perfectly respectable position. That sort of thinking had not only inspired much of the Plowden Report on primary education, it had been responsible for the millions of pounds invested in Western-type education in the newly independent countries of the Third World. Thousands of teachers, too, who were not necessarily as extreme in their methods, were concerned that schools should exist to serve not just the average and above-average, but also, and perhaps especially, the below average. Interestingly, by the time they came to give evidence at the inquiry, both Mr Ellis and Mr Haddow had adopted the position which has come to be associated with Christopher Jenks, following the publication in 1974 of his book *Inequality* – namely, that as agents of social change, schools and education were non-starters. However many resources were poured into them, schools just did not make that much difference to the life chances of the disadvantaged children. Whatever the rights and wrongs of that controversy, few people, whether parents, teachers or educationists, have ever behaved as though schools did not affect society. Most people, though, being naturally conservative, wanted them to buttress the society they knew rather than change it into something they did not; if change was to come, they wanted it brought about by mature minds which had been educated to be critical while at school – a very different proposition from the radical one.

Another view was that schools existed not to change society, but to prepare for change. The world was changing very much faster than in previous generations, and it was a reasonable prediction that the rate of change would go on accelerating. Technology that was taught in schools today would be out of date tomorrow, and would in any case be too much for any one individual to master. The world of tomorrow was bound to be a world of group activity and co-operative projects and it was important that children be prepared for a world of continuous adaptation. All questions of social reform apart, co-operative informal teaching methods would be more suitable for that purpose than formal, traditional ones.

Either of these approaches – changing society or preparing society for change – was bound to make exceptionally heavy demands on the teachers. The great innovators in education were all exceptionally gifted pedagogues. At William Tyndale, there were a few good teachers but that was not enough, even if it had been supplemented by the diligence and enthusiasm which many teachers show, on which to build the ambitious programme the staff had in mind. Teacher training, too often thought of as a panacea, could make little difference, as colleges of education were limited both by the quality of the students they received (Mr Ellis was one of the very few graduates in primary teaching) and by the intrinsic difficulty of teaching people how to teach. All they could do was to provide their students with a minimum of further education, a few good ideas for progressive teaching and one or two basic techniques of classroom control which it was hoped would act as a safety net.

What was left, then, as an aim of primary education? Once the 11-plus had gone, there was no measure of achievement at all, however unsatisfactory. Children moved on up into secondary schools when they were 11 or 12, whether or not they had learnt how to read or write; there was no question of keeping anyone back. The notion, popular among parents, that children should be taught the 'basics' while at primary school was the only hint of a minimum standard. Even that, though, if it were to be formalised, would require some form of attainment testing, and since the abolition of the 11-plus it had become impossible for educationists to reach agreement among themselves on a value-free objective test – or even on the merits of testing at all.

Assessment   It is difficult to talk of assessing the performance of teachers when there is no agreement on what teachers are supposed to be doing. In the absence of any agreed criteria all that is possible is for professional experts to go into a school, look at what the teachers were doing, talk to the teachers themselves about it, and then make their own assessment. That is what a full inspection was all about. But there was no basis on which one school could be compared with another – except the subjective impressions of the inspectors, a group of men or women whose sole qualification for the job was that they had once been good teachers. Moreover, the touchiness of many teachers and their unions, concerned with their status as qualified professionals and therefore not subject to outside control (though, as we saw, the NUT would not go against the law), contributed to the general unwillingness of the inspectors to force their opinions down anybody's throat.

Another factor at work here was what one might term the unacceptable face of authority. Research evidence suggests that both parents and children like teachers to be tough, authoritarian figures but, like social workers, teachers had come increasingly to think of themselves – and be thought of by others – as one of the 'caring professions'. That meant, in this context, that they did not make 'judgements' about their 'clients', whether they were incontinent old men, dangerous juvenile delinquents or backward schoolchildren; all they did was make the non-moral assessments that were necessary for them to do their job. But what was true for their clients had also become true for themselves. Together with the fashion for participation and democratic decision making in everything (and not just politics), that meant that it had become virtually impossible for anybody who had a position of responsibility in the hierarchy to say: you are doing your job badly – do it better or get out. Soft-centred liberals should remember that more revolutions have failed through inefficiency than for any other single cause.

Inspectors, therefore, preferred the role of adviser. In fact, rather than see themselves as the shock troops who could be sent in at the slightest hint of trouble, they preferred the image of staff officers, helping, advising, prodding the troops in the front line, but rarely taking the field themselves. They saw themselves rather as a teaching elite; knowing that there were not enough of them to go round every school, they tried to spread their qualities as wide as possible by working at one remove through the classroom teachers. There was certainly a case for that, just as there was a case for fewer, better-trained teachers and more untrained (and less expensive) teacher aides.

But if inspectors abandoned their role of assessors, who was to make judgements about how well or badly teachers might be doing their job? The teachers themselves? The ILEA inspectorate, at least, would like to evolve some formula for teacher self-assessment. Curiously, however, that is something teachers themselves have not pressed for. Despite their oft-repeated concern for their professional status, they have been strangely unpreoccupied with some of the things that would give meaning to that status, such as control of the qualifications for entry into the profession, or the sort of freedom from the judgement of outsiders that is enjoyed by doctors and lawyers. Both these professions have some sort of council which hears and judges claims of professional misconduct. The teachers have never pressed for a general teaching council along the same lines.

Indeed, one of the points to emerge most strongly from any discussion of the issues raised by William Tyndale was the ambiguous nature of teachers' claims to professional status. Certainly, there were ways in which teachers could justifiably claim that they adopted a professional attitude to their work, but the fact that in other respects society was not prepared to grant them that status was symptomatic of something very important. A doctor's clinical judgement is just that: a judgement of fact and diagnosis about clinical matters. A teacher's judgements are made about values, and very fundamental ones at that. Those sort of judgements were thought to be too important to be left to teachers alone.

Accountability   But by the same token, as the story of William Tyndale amply illustrated, nobody else was willing to take on the responsibility for the judgements – and performance – of teachers. If nothing was done about it, sooner or later market forces would begin to take a hand, as in a sense they did at William Tyndale when parents began to vote with their feet by taking their children away. There were already pressures, by those involved in educational politics on the extreme left as well as the extreme right, for this sort of parental assessment to be institutionalised – say, through a voucher system, under which parents would be given an educational ticket for each of their children which they could cash at the school of their choice. Schools would then be competing with one another for clients, just as they do already in the private sector. But that would have several disadvantages, the major one of which is common to all solutions that involve the undifferentiated voice of parents or the community. Everybody has been to school, but nobody has ever learnt anything about education there. If it was wrong, as it surely was, to leave teachers free to exercise their uncontrolled will on children, then it was also wrong to leave decisions about the type of education children should receive to parents with the sort of views we encountered in Chapter 4.

That left some sort of representative community control – which of course had been the thinking behind the institution of managers and governors in the first place. However, as we have seen, under that system managers left a lot to be desired, in terms of both their appointment and their competence. One solution might have been for them to be directly elected at the same time as local councillors. But however they might be appointed, they had to know something about education and educational issues so that, if teachers or the headteacher wanted to introduce new policies into the school, they would have to justify them to the managers – but to managers who would be reasonably well informed.

All these issues we have mentioned – the powers and responsibilities of local authorities, the control of the curriculum, the criteria for assessing a school's efficiency, the aims of primary education, the need for testing, the role of the inspectorate, the function of managers and the professionalism and accountability of teachers – are proper subjects for consideration by the Secretary of State for Education. Only he can see that the lessons of William Tyndale are, where appropriate, applied nationally and only he is in a position to assess the implications for bodies such as the Schools Council. But above all, only the Secretary of

State can take an overview of the issue which underlies every other: the proper balance to be struck between politicians and the community on the one hand, and teachers and the other professionals on the other. After William Tyndale, the Secretary of State can no longer pretend, as he and his predecessors have so often tended to do, that it is all happening somewhere else.